Structural Exegesis:
From Theory to Practice

Structural Exegesis: From Theory to Practice

Exegesis of Mark 15 and 16
Hermeneutical Implications

DANIEL PATTE
ALINE PATTE

FORTRESS PRESS   PHILADELPHIA

For our children

Murielle, David, *and* Chantal

Library of Congress Cataloging in Publication Data

Patte, Daniel.
   Structural exegesis: from theory to practice.

   Includes bibliographical references and index.
   1. Bible—Hermeneutics.   2. Structuralism
(Literary analysis)   I. Patte, Aline, joint author.
II. Title.
BS476.P33   220.6'3   78-54557
ISBN 0-8006-0524-1

7132D88   Printed in the United States of America   1–524

Contents

Preface

The present book aims at establishing a fully operational method of structural exegesis. The readers of *What Is Structural Exegesis?* are aware of the need for such a work! Part of the "Guides to Biblical Scholarship" series, that book outlines in a theoretical argument the promises that structuralism holds for biblical exegesis. According to these methodological reflections, it appeared that one can expect structural exegesis to provide an important complement to traditional exegesis and in so doing help bridge the gap between the exegesis and the hermeneutics of the biblical text. Yet the main results of structuralist research in linguistics, literary studies, and anthropology presented in the rest of that volume proved disappointing as far as a hope for a full-blown exegetical method is concerned.

While this threefold research clearly appeared as the basis upon which methods of structural exegesis could be developed, it was also clear that the mere application of the methods of analysis used in literary structuralism and in anthropological structuralism was not yet yielding much exegetical fruit. Reflecting the status of the research, this presentation remained open-ended. It was suggested that structural exegesis could eventually be used for the study of various features of a text such as its narrative system, its literary genre, its mythical system, its semantic system. But it remained to determine which types of study would best help fulfill the exegetical promises of structural research. It was also suggested that before establishing a method of exegesis (for the study of what characterizes a given text) further fundamental structural research (focused on the study of the phenomenon of communication in general) was needed. More specifically, the relations among narrative, mythical, and semantic structures had to be ascertained so as to provide criteria for the control of the analysis at these three levels. A tentative model of the relations between mythical and narrative structures was proposed in a brief statement (p. 78) as an expression of a methodological investigation in progress that we will need to revise quite radically (see below, Chapter 2).

Despite its limitations, *What Is Structural Exegesis?* has hopefully helped readers to become aware of the promises of structural research for biblical exegesis and also to acquire a structuralist (or semiotic) vision of the meaning of a text as "meaning effect" which can be deconstructed into its narrative, mythical, and semantic components. These are the necessary first steps into structural exegetical studies. The present book builds upon this basis and therefore presupposes the reading of *What Is Structural Exegesis?*

Our first task was to determine which specific goal would be the most appropriate for a first structural exegetical method. Considering both the nature of structural methods and our exegetical needs, we opted for the development of a method which would permit the rigorous study of the system of "values" *presupposed* by a text (and that one might want to call a system of convictions, as will be explained below). This option will allow us to focus our study on features that are specific to a given text. Yet these values should not be construed as part of the content of the meaning of the text (this conception would imply an understanding of meaning as the content found in the text-container!). Rather, they are the semantic basis (or framework) upon which (in which) the discourse of the text unfolds as a meaningful discourse. Yet the same system of deep values can be the basis of a plurality of meaningful discourses: the text is only one of its possible actualizations. We shall see that the legitimate herme-neutics of the text are new discourses which use as a semantic basis (or framework) the same system of deep values as the text (see Chapter 4). By elucidating the system of values presupposed by a text, we will therefore determine the basis (or framework) upon which (in which) the various legitimate hermeneutical discourses of this text should unfold. In brief, the believers for whom this text is "Scripture" or "canon" should have discourses and lives presupposing and manifesting the same convictions as the text.

This goal being set, it remained to establish a rigorous method for the study of this dimension of the meaning effect. For this purpose we could not rely on the results of existing structuralist research; there was no fully satisfactory theory (or model) explaining the relationship between the system of values presupposed by a text and the surface textual manifesta-tion (which has to be the starting point of any exegesis). We had no other alternative than to involve ourselves in theoretical structuralist and semiotic research so as to contribute to the study of this specific aspect of the phe-nomenon of communication. More precisely, on the basis of the works of

Lévi-Strauss, Greimas, and their collaborators, we had to address the question of the relations between the syntagmatic and the paradigmatic organizations of discourses as macro-signs. The model proposed in Chapter 2 is our contribution to fundamental structuralist research on the semiotics of discourse in general. Its presentation and justification demand a very abstract and involved argument in implicit and explicit dialogue with various semiotic and structuralist studies. We invite the readers to follow the suggestions of the notes, which propose at various points to intersperse in the reading of this theoretical chapter the reading of concrete examples from the exegesis of Mark 15 and 16 in Chapter 3. The very precision (and complexity) of this theoretical model allows us to derive from it an exegetical method which is well defined and therefore relatively easy to use with the necessary rigor. In fact, one can begin to use this method with satisfactory exegetical results even before fully understanding its theoretical justification (as undergraduate freshmen have done in one of my classes). At any rate, readers need not wait for a full understanding of Chapter 2 before proceeding with the reading of Chapter 3. The latter chapter reaches significant exegetical conclusions that are meaningful in and of themselves.

While the entire book is indeed the result of our joint research and writing, Daniel Patte is more directly responsible for the theoretical chapters (Chapters 1, 2, and 4), while Aline Patte is more directly responsible for the exegesis of Mark 15 and 16 (Chapter 3). This chapter is in fact an abridged and translated version of the thesis she presented as partial fulfillment of the requirements for the *Maîtrise en Théologie* that she received *summa cum laude* from the Institut Protestant de Théologie (Paris) in June 1977.

Once more this work springs from the interdisciplinary seminars that gather together the Structuralist Research Group at Vanderbilt University, including at present J. R. Andrews (Spanish and Portuguese), J. L. Crenshaw (Old Testament), L. S. Crist (French), J. E. Engel (German), W. von Raffler Engel (Linguistics), R. K. Gottfried (English), C. Hasenmueller (Fine Arts), J. F. Parker (Computer Science and Religion), R. A. Peterson (Sociology), J. F. Plummer (English), C. E. Scott (Philosophy), and L. H. Silberman (Jewish Studies). It is with gratitude that we acknowledge here that each has contributed in one way or another to this book by his or her probing questions and suggestions.

Our gratitude goes also to Pierre Geoltrain (Professor at l'École des Hautes Études, Paris), Jean Delorme (Professor at the Catholic University, Lyon), and A. J. Greimas (Professor at l'École des Hautes Études, Paris) who have graciously invited Daniel Patte to present preliminary versions of the methodological part of this book in their respective seminars and have facilitated in this way the development of a more rigorous theory and method. In addition, Professor Greimas was kind enough to read and criticize a first draft of Chapter 2. While we hope to have corrected the errors and weaknesses that he noted, we must nevertheless assume the full responsibility for the content of this chapter. In the context of another seminar at Vanderbilt, Neil Christy, Alan Conrath, Karl Plank, and Gary Patterson have contributed to a first sketch of the exegesis of Mark 15 and 16 (establishment of the narrative hierarchy) while making valuable methodological suggestions. Last but not least, our gratitude goes to John Jones and Gary Phillips, who have helped us put various parts of this text into English. Because this book is simultaneously published in English and in French (*Pour une Exégèse Structurale* [Paris: Seuil, 1978], which also includes a translation of *What Is Structural Exegesis?*), some of its chapters have first been written in French, others in English.

It is our pleasant duty to acknowledge the financial support provided for the preparation of this book by the Research Council of Vanderbilt University and the Association of Theological Schools through the fellowships they granted to Daniel Patte, and by the National Endowment for the Humanities through a collective Pilot Program Grant given to the Structuralist Research Group at Vanderbilt University. This book, together with the Computer Assisted Instruction modules prepared on its basis by a team under the leadership of J. F. Parker, will hopefully help the teaching of structuralist exegetical methods in undergraduate as well as divinity school classes.

DANIEL AND ALINE PATTE

Vanderbilt University
June 1978

1

A Specific Goal
for Structural Exegesis

Structural exegesis is characterized by a rigorous method that at first seems quite complex. It is indeed a sophisticated analytical tool, as is any exegetical method. Yet performing a good structural exegesis is certainly no more difficult than doing a good form-critical or redaction-critical study. One could even contend that it is simpler, because the exegesis can be performed by following a series of well-defined steps. The structural exegetical methods presented in *What Is Structural Exegesis?*[1] and in the present book might initially *appear* to be very—and perhaps excessively—complex. Yet, it is only an *appearance* of complexity that we need to dispel.

Structuralist methods seem to be more complicated than other exegetical methods because they involve, for the exegete, a shift in paradigm. Instead of being built upon the historical paradigm as are most other exegetical methods, structuralist methods follow a linguistic paradigm. Confronted by structuralist methods, the traditional exegete is in a situation similar to that of a person confronted for the first time with a foreign language. This language is meaningless and *seems* much more complex than one's mother tongue. When one has at last mastered this new language one then realizes that its difficulty is comparable to that of any other language. This analogy also implies that learning how to use structural methods is somewhat similar to learning a foreign language: it is painstaking! Now this raises a question: Is it worthwhile to learn these new methods?

Structuralist methods often appear excessively complex in comparison to the results one can expect from their use. This feeling results in part from the process through which these exegetical methods were developed. The scholars who first involved themselves in structuralist research did not know precisely what the usefulness of this research would be. They were simply convinced that somehow a study of texts in terms of the increasing knowledge about the phenomenon of human communication would be

1

useful. Essay after essay was published pointing out various possible goals and methods. At last the dust is beginning to settle and the hope of the pioneers is being vindicated. It is now clear that structuralist methods permit for the first time the systematic study of important dimensions of the meaning of texts and other cultural phenomena.

Yet these dimensions of meaning are difficult to name and to describe because we are not used to considering them in and of themselves. Our situation is somewhat similar to that of those scientists who used microscopes and saw for the first time microscopic living organisms and particles. They did not have any precise names for them because up until then they were only conceived as features of macroscopic phenomena. Similarly, structuralist research as part of the research on the phenomenon of communication gives us a new "vision"[2] of the meaning of a text. Instead of perceiving it as an entity, we perceive it as a "meaning effect"[3] of which we can distinguish several dimensions.[4]

INFORMATIONAL AND SYMBOLIC
DIMENSIONS OF MEANING

We must first distinguish between the "informational" and "symbolic" dimensions of the meaning of a text. This fundamental distinction is both similar to and different from the one we commonly recognize between "plain speech" and "symbolic speech" (such as poetry). Robert Tannehill provides us with a clear description of the contrasting features of these two types of speech.[5]

"Plain speech" is primarily "informational," in the sense that its function is the communication of data and other pieces of information. These include information about the concreteness of human experience (e.g., things, personages, events, situations) as well as about the abstract realm of ideas (e.g., doctrines and theories such as philosophical and theological views, ethical values and principles). In terms of its function, "plain speech" (which has many different forms) is "related to decision and action."[6] Using A. J. Greimas's actantial terminology, it is the communication of HELPERS for the SUBJECT, the communication of data that gives "power" and "know-how" to the subject and that opens up the possibility of carrying out various somatic or cognitive actions. This kind of speech communicates ideas, ethical values and principles (eventually expressed in the form of suggestions or even commands) which contribute to decision processes, that is, to the establishment of the volition of the SUBJECT. In order to perform these functions efficiently, "plain speech" must be clear and precise, logical and unambiguous.

In contrast to "plain speech" Tannehill opposes "symbolic speech," which he terms "forceful and imaginative language." Its function is not the communication of data but the communication of visions of life and of the world. It opens a window upon the realm of feelings (which manifest the values that we spontaneously attach to the interrelationship of the innumerable facets of human experience) and upon the realm of the imagination (through which we perceive the fundamental purposefulness and meaningfulness of life). The main function of symbolic speech is the awakening of the imagination by challenging (or eventually reinforcing) the vision of life and of the world that we hold. In order to perform this function, imaginative language is characterized by a use of words that emphasizes their connotations; the words have, therefore, a "soft focus" and "blurred edges" because of the "connotative fringe" that they carry.[7] This imaginative language is also qualified by Tannehill as being "forceful"; it has the *power* to awaken the imagination, the power to "touch the depths from which our personal visions of life arise."[8]

In contrast to Tannehill's distinction between informational language (plain speech) and symbolic (imaginative) language, we propose a distinction between the informational and symbolic dimensions of the meaning of a text (or language). In other words, we want to stress that any speech or text has both an informational and a symbolic function. The difference between informational and symbolic language is only relative; it is a matter of the emphasis put on one or the other function. Informational language emphasizes the denotative (or referential) dimension of its meaning and does not call attention to its symbolic (or connotative) dimension, while symbolic language does the reverse.[9] Similarly, since texts or speeches can be viewed as macro-signs, we cannot accept the view (such as Tillich's[10]) that holds sign and symbol to be fundamentally different. A symbol as well as a sign has both a denotative-referential dimension (it points to "something") and a connotative-symbolic dimension (its "value," in Ferdinand de Saussure's terminology). The difference between sign and symbol is a matter of emphasis. For instance, the sign "typewriter" refers to this machine on the desk (denotative dimension), yet it also has various connotations such as "technological," "educational," "modern." In everyday speech we would ignore these connotations, even though they remain part of the signified (or content) of the sign. By contrast, when considering a symbol we are primarily aware of its connotations (e.g., the cross represents "salvation"; the flag, the "nation" or "patriotism"), while we have a tendency to ignore its denotative meaning (the cross refers to Jesus' crucifixion; the American flag with its stars and stripes refers to the States and the Colonies).

TOWARD A SYSTEMATIC STUDY OF
SYMBOLIC DIMENSIONS OF MEANING

On the basis of the preceding distinction we can now formulate the goal of structural exegesis as *the systematic study of symbolic or connotative dimensions of the meaning of a text*. While traditional exegetical methods are primarily suited for the rigorous study of the informational content of a text (e.g., historical references, theological views, "what the author meant to say" through his logical argument), structural methods are uniquely suited for the rigorous study of the symbolic content of a text (whether the text is "imaginative" or "informational" in character) but cannot do anything else. After a complete structural exegesis of a text, we will not understand any better what the author refers to. Our understanding of the historical events unfolding in the Gospel story (or of the surface logic of the argument of Paul's letters) will not have improved. A disappointing performance from the standpoint of traditional exegesis! Yet we will know something about the symbolic dimension of the meaning of this text—the system of values presupposed by the text, a part of the vision of life that the author held.

In studying the symbolic dimension of the meaning of a text, we deal with one of its essential, though neglected, components: the locus of the *power* of the text. Whether a power for awakening the imagination to new (or renewed) visions of life, or a power for putting the imagination to sleep through the constant repetition of old visions, this mysterious power of the text is the key to successful communication. We "receive" the information and make use of it, and we accept a command if, and only if, the text (or speech) has exerted its power upon us, that is, if we share in the vision of life of the text.[11] Hidden within the power of the text is the very possibility of hermeneutic, and also of communication, because it is the "condition of possibilities of a discourse."[12] *It is this power of the text that is the object of the structural exegesis proposed here* as well as in certain other types of structuralist research. Reviewing what some scholars have to say about this power will help us define its nature and thus the goal of our structural exegesis.

SYMBOLIC MEANING AS POWER

In the explanation of the approach and the goal of a new study that will unfold in several volumes, Michel Foucault in *La volonté de savoir*[13] states that he intends to deal with that which has actual power upon people. For him this power resides neither in the politicians nor in the experts who govern the political and economic life of a nation. Instead it is an enigmatic and mysterious reality that is at once visible and invisible, present and hidden in a society's life as a whole. From Foucault's preceding books[14] we know that when speaking of "power" he refers to a system of deep values, sometimes termed *episteme,* which both governs and results from our "gaze" (French: *regard*) upon life and the world.

Similarly, Roland Barthes in his opening lecture at Le Collège de France[15] makes constant use of the term "power," which he associates with a political terminology. It is a power that is neither reactionary nor progressivist but squarely fascist. Yet he speaks not of a political power but of the power of a natural language, an invisible power that imposes upon its users a specific view of the world, a specific way of thinking, of speaking, of being in relation with others. This alienating power of language must be overcome. This is the task that literature performs—or should perform.

Thus Foucault and Barthes, who are both strongly influenced by structuralist research, describe the ultimate object of their research in political terms as a "power." This is a departure from the traditional formulation of the same object in linguistic terms as a system of "deep values" ("value" being understood in de Saussure's sense[16]). This change in terminology reveals that, for various reasons, these two scholars have renounced the development of rigorous structuralist methods; they have freed themselves from the linguistic model. Yet their formulation is helpful and illuminating in the present highly politicized French cultural context. It accurately describes the ultimate object of Claude Lévi-Strauss's and A. J. Greimas's structuralist research, which was so often misunderstood in its linguistic formulation.

Lévi-Strauss, in his study of the deep values that form the mythical system presupposed by a myth, aims indeed at describing what has power upon the collective author and upon those for whom this myth is an integral part of their life.

Upon consideration of the end result of Greimas's recent analyses of texts,[17] it appears that these studies aim at elucidating what he terms the "semantic universe" of the text. It is the "axiological" system of values[18] presupposed by the text and by its author, a system that has power upon the author and eventually upon the reader.

Power as a political metaphor is, therefore, adequate as an expression of the goal of structuralist analysis in the French context. A comparable metaphor for the biblical scholar, and one which will be even more illuminating, is the formulation of this goal in terms of "religious power."

THE POWER OF SYSTEMS OF CONVICTIONS

The term "power" has been used in defining the phenomenon of religion. Thus F. Streng[19] writes: "Religion is a means of ultimate transformation." It is an effective power. "The focus on religion as effective power . . . stresses the recognition by religious adherents that their symbols, techniques and social expressions are not just wishes, hopes and fantasies: rather these are practical means of transforming life from unreality to reality."[20] Thus "the practical power of religion . . . is a power of ultimate reality."[21] Furthermore, Streng defines myth and ritual as "the 'power unto salvation,' the dynamic power embodied in language and gesture that manifests the eternal reality in everyday existence."[22]

While this power has no existence outside of its symbolic manifestations (in the symbols, myths, rituals of a specific religion), it can be described as that part of a system of deep values which, in religious terms, we can call a *system of convictions*. Here, with Cornelius Loew,[23] we use the term "conviction" in its etymological sense of a "value which imposes itself upon the believer as a self-evident truth." Convictions should not, therefore, be confused with "ideas," "doctrines," "ethical values," or "beliefs," which are all the informational, logical content of discourse (and of thought) that can be communicated directly through the denotative function of language. Convictions as *self-evident truths* are necessarily communicated indirectly through the symbolic, connotative function of language. Otherwise they would lose their self-evidence and would become demonstrable, logical truths.

Thus we can further formulate *the ultimate goal of structuralist research as the attempted description of the system of deep values, or convictions, which imposes itself upon people and has the power of transforming unreality into reality for them.* Presupposed by any cultural activity and by any discourse (profane as well as religious), these systems of convictions are the framework within which our discourses and our lives meaningfully unfold. They are, in Foucault's language, the conditions of the possibility of our discourses and lives. Religious manifestations (whether in the form of rituals, myths, or sacred texts) have, in addition, the role of establishing and transmitting these systems of convictions. Their self-evidence and their power are then acknowledged in traditional religious terms when we speak of *revelation*.[24] In other words, applied to biblical texts, we can claim that a structural exegesis aims at describing what was apprehended as revealed, self-evident truth by the authors of these biblical texts. This is what we shall term the system of symbolic values presupposed by a biblical text, or its semantic universe.

The symbolic values that form the semantic universe and that have the power of transforming unreality into reality are complex semantic units manifested by macro-signs, such as narratives. Together these broad semantic units make up the framework in which finer semantic units can find their place. We refer in this instance to the finer symbolic features manifested and established by the linguistic system of signs. The method of structural exegesis proposed below will aim exclusively at elucidating the system of broad symbolic values: the system of convictions presupposed by a text, its semantic universe.

STRUCTURAL METHODS AND THE STUDY
OF SYMBOLIC VALUES

In order to understand why structuralist methods are well suited for the study of the convictions—or the vision of life or again the semantic universe—presupposed by a text, we need to come back briefly to the linguistic model upon which these methods are based.[25]

The content (or signified) of a sign is twofold: its referential-denotative dimension and its symbolic-connotative dimension (its deep value). Both are closely interrelated yet can be distinguished for analytical purposes. The latter is established by the interrelation of the sign with the other signs of the system to which it belongs. On this basis one can understand why the system of symbolic-connotative values forms a semantic universe. Through their referential-denotative function, signs (be they linguistic signs or macro-signs, such as narratives) refer to various elements of the physical world and of human experience. These signs are organized into various systems so as to make possible human communication. This organization of the signs into systems involves the correlated organization of the referential-denotative elements (the raw data of human experience) that are in this way manifested as having specific symbolic values. Through the interaction of the various systems of signs that one uses (the linguistic system, the narrative system, etc.), the raw data of the world and of life are then apprehended as a meaningful world and a purposeful process. *The use of specific systems of signs provides a specific vision of life and of the world.* This meaningful order as a system of symbolic values is the subconscious framework within which the user of these systems of signs lives and thinks; it is a "semantic universe," as Greimas terms it. It provides the basic motivations without which life would be meaningless and purposeless.

We want simply to affirm that systems of symbolic values are manifested through systems of signs. We leave open the question of determining whether the organization of a given system of signs results from a previously accepted system of symbolic values (thereby revelation becomes a possibility) or whether a system of symbolic values merely results from the systems of signs that we have haphazardly adopted as our own. In our view the question of knowing which came first, system of symbolic values or system of signs, can only be resolved on a convictional basis. By contrast, the structuralist theory according to which systems of symbolic values are manifested and transmitted through systems of signs can be verified; it is a valid representation of an aspect of the phenomenon of communication because it can be applied to the study of any narrative (and logical) texts. Let us also note that systems of symbolic values are by nature dynamic and not static. As our systems of signs constantly change—through the incorporation of new signs and the "forgetting" of others—our semantic universe is modified. Still, it is legitimate to make a static description of the semantic universe presupposed and manifested by a text because a text is a frozen speech. We shall suggest how it regains its dynamism in the hermeneutical process.

THE PLACE OF OUR METHOD IN STRUCTURAL RESEARCH

In the preceding pages we have referred to two types of systems: the "systems" of signs and the "systems" of symbolic values. We have noted that they are correlated. But they should not be identified one with the other. Similarly, the structures that govern the organization of their respective elements are distinct even though they are correlated. We shall see that they can be viewed as two distinct levels of the same structural network. Both of these structures are semiotic structures, that is, structures which organize systems of signs at various levels.

In turn these semiotic structures[26] should not be confused with other types of structures, such as "literary structures" (surface organization of a text) and what we would call "semantic frameworks." We need to discuss briefly the latter, because a great deal of confusion was generated in structuralist research due to the lack of clear distinction between "semiotic structures" and "semantic frameworks," also termed "structures" by some authors.

Systems of symbolic values can be viewed as "semantic frameworks" because they function as the basis on which meaningful discourses and lives can unfold. While the ultimate goal of structuralist studies is the study of the systems of symbolic values, such studies are termed "structuralist" not because of this goal but because they pursue this goal with methods based upon the "semiotic structures," that is to say, upon the formal networks of relations which characterize the systems of signs.

Thus, Michel Foucault refuses to be called a structuralist because he does not believe that the linguistic model can be used for the study of the system of symbolic values that characterizes a culture. His methodology is not directly derived from semiotic theories. Similarly, Roland Barthes is no longer a structuralist. Despite the fact that, at first, he worked enthusiastically for the development of structuralist and semiotic methods, he has now abandoned this type of research. In the opening pages of his book *S/Z*[27] he states that despite his former hopes it is impossible to develop structuralist methods for the study of literature. He denies the possibility of establishing a universal network of relations characteristic of narratives (as signs of a system of macro-signs). In his view, even if this could be established it would simply be trivial. What is fascinating, says Barthes, is not the common features that they share but their differences and the plurality of meanings that each has. His recent lecture, briefly discussed above, makes it clear that for him the primary role of literature is iconoclastic with respect to the power of language. Without denying this role to certain types of literature, we must emphasize against Barthes that literature can also have the role of establishing and reenforcing semantic universes. When studying religions we cannot but be aware of this function of stories and scriptures, which can best be explained if stories are viewed as macro-signs. The iconoclastic role of literature can then be looked at as the confrontation of an established semantic universe by a new semantic universe manifested in literature.

We agree with Barthes, however, that the ultimate goal of exegesis is to make clear the specificity and the plurality of meanings of each text. A semantic universe is on the one hand one of the most characteristic features of a given text and on the other hand the basis upon which a plurality of hermeneutical discourses can unfold. Indeed, our structural exegesis pursues the very goal that Barthes sets for himself. Yet, unlike him, we intend to pursue this goal with the help of structuralist methods in order to have as much control as possible over our exegesis. It is for the purpose of developing these methods that the patient study of features common to all narratives—the universal semiotic structures—is necessary. Before the *applied* research aimed at the study of specific features of texts can take place, a *fundamental* research is required.

Greimas and his collaborators have accepted the challenge of establishing the narrative structures, that is, the network of relations (or "gram-

mar") common to any meaningful narrative. The object of this fundamental research is the universal phenomenon of narrativity. For this
purpose Greimas has developed specific methods of analysis that are well
adapted to meeting the goal of elucidating universal structures: *methods
of fundamental research.* On the basis of the knowledge of the universal
structures established with the help of these methods, *methods of applied
research* can and must be developed for the study of what is specific about
a text.

Fundamental structuralist research is still in process. After having
made important progress in the study of the narrative structure, Greimas
dealt with its relation to logical discourses (especially scholarly discourses)[28] before returning to aspects of narrative structure in his latest
seminars. Pierre Geoltrain,[29] Jean Calloud,[30] and Jean Delorme,[31] to
name only three French biblical scholars, are themselves involved in fundamental research focused on the phenomenon of narrativity and also on
the phenomenon of the religious discourse.[32] These various types of
fundamental research aim at showing *how* texts "make sense," that is,
what are the "mechanisms" through which a text is meaningful.

Despite the fact that our primary goal is the development of methods
of applied research, our interdisciplinary research team at Vanderbilt University has necessarily been involved in fundamental research. The second
chapter of this book presents the results of fundamental research on the
interrelation of the narrative structure, the mythical structure, and the
semantic structure. On this basis we are able to establish a method of
applied research, an exegetical method. Our third chapter is an application of this method to Mark 15 and 16. Of course, it can be viewed as a
further verification of the models proposed in the preceding chapter. Yet
the primary goal of this exegesis is the elucidation of the specific semantic
universe presupposed by this text: the system of convictions as manifested
through a symbolic system that is the locus of the "revelatory power" of
this biblical text. As can be expected, this type of study opens up important hermeneutical possibilities, which we shall explore in our last
chapter.

2

From Semiotic Theories
to a Structuralist Method

THE AIM OF THIS THEORETICAL CHAPTER

In *What Is Structural Exegesis?* we have presented the main features of two structures: the narrative and mythical structures (Chapters 3 and 4). In concluding our identification of elements of the mythical system manifested by Galatians 1:1–10, we noted that it would be necessary to go beyond these somewhat imprecise results by proceeding to a semantic analysis which would aim at elucidating the semantic universe presupposed by that text. Thereby structural exegesis would reach its goal. We also suggested the importance of considering the relations between narrative and mythical structures so as to provide criteria for a more rigorous control of the analysis of the mythical system. We concluded with tentative remarks on this subject, illustrated by a study of the parable of the Good Samaritan.

The present chapter proposes for the first time a model that shows the relations among the narrative, mythical, and semantic structures. On the basis of this model it is now possible to envision a method that will enable us to elucidate the semantic universe presupposed by a text by following a series of well-defined analytical steps: (a) The study of the narrative manifestation (the referential-denotative meaning of the story) will enable us to deduce the narrative system of the text. (b) From the study of the narrative system we can deduce the mythical (or symbolic) system. (c) And from the study of the mythical (or symbolic) system, we will be able to deduce the semantic universe. In other words, by employing this method we should be able to describe the system of convictions presupposed by the text with such rigor that two exegetes working independently of each other should reach very similar conclusions.

The strict limitations of the proposed method should be kept in mind: (a) It cannot contribute to a study of the referential-denotative meaning of the text.   In fact, it cannot proceed at all as long as the referential meaning of the text is not established.   The exegete must understand what the text refers to, that is, what a "crowd," a "palace," a "soldier," or a "tomb" is and what the events are which make up the story.   (b) This method attempts to describe the system of broad values that has "power to transform unreality into reality" for the author.   It will allow finer values to slip through its net.   These finer values could be studied with other methods in a linguistic semantic analysis.   (c) Finally, in its present formulation the method is applicable only to narrative texts.   The transposition of this method to the study of logical texts (which we shall only give in outline) is nonetheless easy to imagine.   Yet this method is not applicable to texts of a poetic nature.

The structural model presented here, even though it has been established on the basis of A. J. Greimas's and Claude Lévi-Strauss's works, ventures to some extent into unexplored territories.   We cannot, therefore, merely refer to the research of these scholars for its justification; we will have to provide it.   The arguments justifying this model are necessarily technical and involved.

In order to avoid any misunderstanding, one last remark about the nature of this model is in order.   This model makes no pretense of being an objective description of the manner in which aspects of the meaning of a narrative are produced and apprehended by the human mind; it is simply a *representation* of these phenomena.   Indeed, we do not exclude the possibility that other valid theories can be advanced in order to account for the same phenomena (just as there are several valid theories which account for the phenomenon "electricity").   The validity of our model holds insofar as it is operative; regardless of the narrative considered, it is possible to identify the relations that form the structural network described by this model.

The Weaknesses of Existing Models

In order to be in a position to elucidate the mythical system—or more precisely, as we shall see, a *portion* of the mythical system—and beyond that, the semantic universe that a mythological or non-mythological narrative presupposes, we must first establish a model of the relations among the narrative manifestation, the mythical system, and the semantic universe.   In the absence of such a model the analysts find themselves lacking the criteria that would enable them to choose with all necessary rigor the pertinent categories which serve as a basis for the semantic analysis.

In our view, Lévi-Strauss is in just this kind of predicament.   In his pioneering work he often gives the impression of making arbitrary choices even though he has established a number of criteria for controlling his analysis. Those criteria that he derives from a model of the relations between the variants of a myth (his formula) are too general to allow for a rigorous control of the analysis. It must be said though that without the research of Lévi-Strauss the model of the relations between the narrative manifestation and the mythical system described below could not have been established.

Greimas and his collaborators for their part have sought to establish this model through their research upon the narrative structure and the semiotic square[1] without, however, attaining a full formulation of it. The reason for this inconclusive research lies in their concurrent preoccupation with the formulation of models that account for other features of the meaning effect. Consequently, even given the fact that numerous criteria govern their analysis, the choice of categories and pertinent oppositions does not always have the rigor that we have the right to expect of a structural method. The elaboration of this model toward which Greimas and his collaborators work[2] and which we propose below was made possible in the interdisciplinary setting of the Structural Research Group at Vanderbilt University. In this context we were led to examine the theories of Greimas in terms of those of Lévi-Strauss and therefore to concentrate our research upon a very specific aspect of the narrative meaning effect, namely, the relations among narrative manifestation, mythical system, and semantic universe.

Two general remarks will permit us to situate the problems standing before us. First, a mythical system is a paradigmatic system (a system of symbolic values), whereas the narrative manifestation is syntagmatic by nature (the chainlike succession of narrative elements). We must then conceive of the relations between these two systems as similar to those between two planes which we might eventually project one upon the other. What is perceived in one plane as a narrative development (e.g., the performance of a narrative program) is apprehended in the other plane as a mytheme. The "correspondence" of one structural level with another can therefore be viewed as the rule for projecting elements in one plane onto another plane. It is this rule that needs to be defined as precisely as possible.

Secondly, according to Lévi-Strauss's definition, a mythical system is manifested through a series of narratives.[3] Thus a single narrative manifests only certain elements of a mythical system. Lévi-Strauss suggests by his formula that a simple narrative manifests only two oppositions of the mythical system, one opposition being mediated by the other opposition. This second opposition, which is itself mediated, is alone expressed in narrative form; the first opposition is expressed merely in a symbolic form. What then, we ask, are the narrative elements that correspond to the terms of the opposition of the mythical structure expressed in narrative form?

Some scholars have proposed that the macro-mythemes correspond to the symbolic values of the correlated contents—the situation of lack and that of the liquidated lack—with their mediating term being the topical content.[4] We must take exception to this model because it in effect reduces the mythical structure to the narrative structure and thereby confuses a paradigmatic with a syntagmatic system. In the final analysis two types of oppositions are confused with one another: the contrary oppositions are confused with the contradictory oppositions. As underscored by Greimas, we may say that the mythical and narrative structures (or metalanguages) "are *equivalents* because they are isotopic but not isomorphic, indicating thereby that a determined segment of one metalanguage (or structure) can be transcoded into an isotopic segment of another (metalanguage or structure), even though the constitutive elements of the two segments are not formally identical."[5]

We must also refine the model which, in the concluding part of Chapter 4 of *What Is Structural Exegesis?* we proposed as a working hypothesis still undergoing verification. According to this model, the symbolic value of the *situation of lack* was viewed as being opposed to the symbolic value of the *hero* (the SUBJECT of the topical program as defined by its relation to other actantial positions, especially that of the HELPER and by the functions that it performs). The situation of *"non-lack"* (of liquidated lack) was then viewed as the mediating term of the previous opposition. Therefore, the hero would represent the pole $F_x(b)$ and the situation of lack the pole $F_{a-1}(y)$. In practice this model was shown to be inadequate for two main reasons. First, the category "situation of lack" (taken over from Propp's analysis of Russian folktales) is extremely difficult to define with any accuracy. Moreover, and this is the crucial point, the model was not operative. Although it was adequate for the analysis of some very simple narratives such as parables, it has proved itself only approximate and therefore not very useful in the analysis of more complex narratives. In reality, each term (e.g., $F_x[a]$) of Lévi-Strauss's formula represents a macro-mytheme or "bundle of mythemes" and *not a mytheme,* whereas the narrative elements correspond to mythemes. In a very simple narrative each "bundle of mythemes" may eventually be manifested by a single mytheme. But as soon as the narrative becomes more complex this identification of macro-mythemes with mythemes is no longer possible.

It is only proper, therefore, to revise this model quite radically so as to formulate in a more precise way the relations between the mythical system (the system of macro-mythemes) and the narrative manifestation by considering an intermediary level—that of the system of *mythemes,* which we will designate as the *symbolic system.* It becomes possible then to enlarge this model in such a way as to account for the relations among narrative manifestation, mythical system, symbolic system, and semantic universe. In the theoretical presentation that follows, this expanded model may appear unduly complex. This results from the fact that it attempts to represent the interrelation of a large number of structural levels. But it is precisely the distinction between these different levels which will enable us to elaborate a relatively simple method by the fact that it decomposes the analytical work into a succession of well-defined procedures.

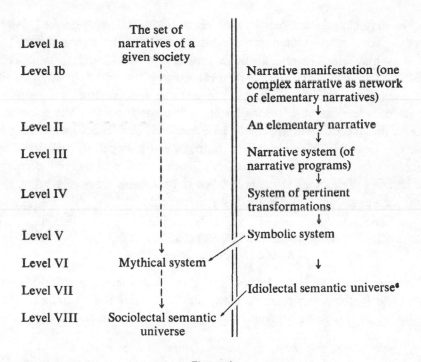

Figure 1

In order to permit the reader to have a preview of the model as a whole, we represent in Figure 1 the different structural levels and their relations. The arrows stand for these relations. But the orientation of these arrows does not imply that certain levels are more important than others; all these structural levels participate concurrently in the production of the meaning effect. The arrows' orientation merely indicates the trajectory that the analysis follows; the dotted arrow represents the path taken by Lévi-Strauss, the solid one the path we shall follow.[7]

How to Read the Following Pages

In the following pages the model in Figure 1 is presented and theoretically justified. This theoretical justification demands an abstract argument that would lose its coherence if it were interrupted with concrete examples. In order to avoid this difficulty, we have supplied a series of notes that refer to Chapter 3. We urge the readers to interrupt their reading as often as necessary in order to follow the suggestions found in the notes. References will be found to concrete illustrations of the points under discussion as presented in the context of the structural exegesis of Mark 15 and 16. In this way parts of Chapter 3 will be read concurrently with Chapter 2.

We may suggest another way of reading the following pages. After studying the various components of this model in the above figure, the readers may elect to read through the description of the method (pp. 36–38) and the example of structural exegesis proposed in Chapter 3. In this way the readers will first apprehend the various structural elements in the concreteness of their manifestation in a specific text. Yet at several points the exegesis will appear to be arbitrary. A subsequent reading of the theoretical justification of the model (which hopefully will have by then lost its abstract character) will allow the readers to understand more completely the exegetical method. While both these ways of reading the following pages are possible, the first is preferable.

MYTHICAL SYSTEM, SYMBOLIC SYSTEM, AND SEMANTIC UNIVERSE

As an initial step, we will consider the relations among mythical system, symbolic system, ideolectal semantic universe, and sociolectal semantic universe. In so doing we will define each of these structural levels.[8]

Mythical System (Level VI) and Symbolic System (Level V)

According to Lévi-Strauss, a mythical system is formed by a series of oppositions of macro-mythemes that are homologous to each other. They are ultimately homologous to the opposition "life vs. death" in that they propose a progressive metaphorical mediation of this fundamental (or existential) opposition. With each macro-mytheme being the semantic value of a bundle of mythemes, we can say that each opposition of the mythical system corresponds to a series of oppositions of mythemes. Consequently we can say that the system of mythemes manifested in a narrative—its symbolic system—is composed of a series of oppositions of mythemes that are homologous to an opposition of macro-mythemes in the mythical system. This already implies that the oppositions of mythemes are homologous to each other. There is no reason to doubt that these homologations obey the same symbolic logic as the one governing the mythical system.[9]

The symbolic system may, therefore, be conceived of as a mythical *micro*-system, a system of homologous oppositions of mythemes that proposes a progressive metaphorical mediation of a "fundamental" opposition which is, in this case, one of the oppositions of macro-mythemes in the mythical system. Consequently the mythical and symbolic systems in and of themselves have the same structure even though their respective semantic investments (macro-mythemes and mythemes) are different. Thus we may say that a mythical system is manifested by a whole series of symbolic systems that only a three-dimensional model allows us to represent.

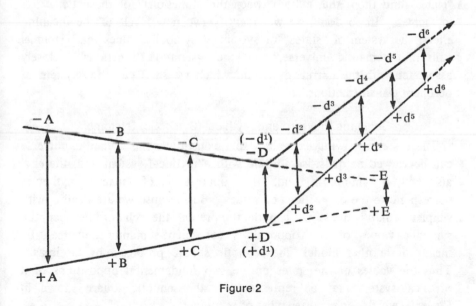

Figure 2

In Figure 2 the oppositions $+A/-A$ . . . $+E/-E$ represent the mythical system (the system of macro-mythemes) that proposes a mediation of the fundamental opposition $+A/-A$. The oppositions $+d^1/-d^1$, $+d^2/-d^2$ . . . represent the symbolic system (the system of mythemes) that proposes a mediation of the opposition of macro-mythemes $+D/-D$.

The structure common to both the mythical and symbolic systems is therefore a series of interrelated oppositions. The relations between two consecutive oppositions that we expressed up to this point with the help of the concepts of "homologation" and "progressive mediation" must now be defined in a more rigorous way.[10]

Lévi-Strauss has made an attempt to account for the relations between two oppositions with his formula $F_x(a) : F_y(b) :: F_x(b) : F_{a-1}(y)$. The complexity of this formula,[11] which renders it virtually unusable, results from the fact that Lévi-Strauss takes into consideration the relations between very complex units. A (macro)-mytheme is composed of a state and a function. Lévi-Strauss is obliged therefore to account simultaneously for three types of relations—the relations between macro-mythemes in each opposition, the relations between the oppositions themselves, and the relations between "state" and "function" within each macro-mytheme —and for the correlation of these three relations. We can see the necessity for simplifying the problem by breaking it down. Instead of considering the relations that exist between (macro)-mythemes in both oppositions, we will consider separately the relations that exist between the "states" and those that exist between the "functions" of these (macro)-mythemes. In so doing we will identify two new levels of the meaning effect: the system of "states" or system of symbolic values that Greimas calls the "semantic universe," and the system of "functions"[12] closely associated with the narrative system, which we shall call the "system of pertinent transformations."

Semantic Universe and Mythical (Symbolic) Systems

The system of symbolic values that constitutes the semantic universe can be viewed as quasi-isomorphic with a mythical system and, thereby, also with a symbolic system. The oppositions of (macro)-mythemes correspond to the oppositions of values. But because we are dealing with simpler semantic units we can then represent the relation between the symbolic values of two oppositions (or micro-semantic universe) by means of another model: the semiotic square proposed by Greimas.[13] Thus the values of the states of the two fundamental oppositions of a mythical system may be represented in the semiotic square shown in Figure 3, which depicts three types of relations:

(1) *The relations of contrariety,* which are manifested in the opposition of the contraries "life vs. death" and in the opposition of the subcontraries "non-death vs. non-life." A relation of contrariety "corresponds" to an opposition of (macro)-mythemes of the mythical (symbolic) struc-

ture. But we should emphasize that the opposition of (macro)-mythemes, which is an opposition of more complex semantic units, cannot be assimilated to an opposition of contraries.

(2) *The relations of contradiction,* which are manifested in the opposi- tions "life vs. non-life" and "death vs. non-death."

(3) *The relations of implication,* which are manifested in the relation between "non-death" and "life" (the semantic category "life" implies the category "non-death") and between "non-life" and "death" (the category "death" implies the category "non-life"). Each of these relations of im- plication, which Greimas calls a "deixis," corresponds to a correlation of (macro)-mythemes in the mythical structure. In the same way that we can distinguish within the mythical (symbolic) structure between a positive axis and a negative axis, so also are we able to distinguish within the square a positive deixis—by convention always to be found on the left—and a negative deixis.

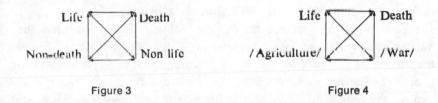

Figure 3   Figure 4

Since a mythical (symbolic) system can be viewed as a *series* of in- terrelated oppositions, the corresponding semantic universe can be viewed as a *series* of semiotic squares. Any consecutive pair of oppositions of a mythical (symbolic) system corresponds to a semiotic square. The differ- ence between mythical and symbolic systems is found in the respective na- tures of the terms. The (macro)-mythemes are complex semantic units— including "states" and "functions." The terms of the semiotic square are "symbolic values" symbolized by the (macro)-mythemes. For example, the square of semantic values in Figure 4 corresponds to the two most funda- mental oppositions of the Zuni myth as interpreted by Lévi-Strauss.[14]

The terms /agriculture/ and /war/ should be read as "values" sym- bolized by the macro-mythemes agriculture and war. Let us stress that these terms represent *not* macro-mythemes (complex semantic units com- bining states and functions) but values symbolized by the states. The value is thus formed by some (and only some) of the semantic features manifested by a (macro)-mytheme. A (macro)-mytheme may be viewed as a symbolic unit, the value of which is manifested by its state.

In order to elucidate the value symbolized by each (macro)-mytheme, we need to identify the semantic features that are pertinent. For this purpose one can make use of the three types of relations that characterize the semiotic square. The pertinent semantic features which form the value /agriculture/ are those that set it in a relation of contradiction with "death," in a relation of implication with "life," and in a relation of contrariety with "war."[15] [Concrete examples are given on pp. 62–90.]

This correspondence between two successive oppositions of the mythical (and symbolic) system and a semiotic square of values will be true if we can account for the mediating process. To repeat once again, it is important not to assimilate "mythical mediation" and "semantic mediation." These two types of mediation correspond to one another but do not belong to the same plane. In the mythical (and symbolic) system, a (macro)-mytheme (war, in the Zuni myth) is the mediating term of the preceding opposition (life vs. death); that is to say, this term is the combination of the semantic features of the two terms of this opposition. This type of mediation is clearly what Lévi-Strauss describes in his study of the Zuni myth; for instance, in the case of the third opposition the scavenger is *both likened* to the herbivore (it does not kill) *and likened* to the predator (it is carnivorous).[16] Let us note that this type of mediation involves the functions ("killing" is clearly a function, "being carnivorous" as "eating meat" is also a function). By contrast, when we consider the values (symbolized by the states) as represented in a semiotic square, we can see that each of the subcontraries (the values of "agriculture" and "war" in the above example) can be considered as a mediating term of the opposition of the contraries. Yet the semantic mediation is not dialectical (its mediating term does not include *both* of the terms of the opposition). The subcontrary is a mediating term in that it gathers together in itself two semantic "fields" (a more precise terminology will be established below). For instance, as the contradictory of /death/, /agriculture/ manifests the semantic field (or, more specifically, as we shall see, the *isotopic space*) /death/ by the very fact that it negates it. Simultaneously, because it is in a relation of implication with /life/, /agriculture/ positively manifests the semantic field (or, more specifically, the *semantic axis*) /life/. Thus, each of the subcontraries is the intersecting point of the semantic fields of the two contraries. The subcontrary of the positive deixis is the one that is posited as the most adequate mediating term.[17]

This representation on a semiotic square of the relations among the values symbolized by the states of two oppositions of the mythical system shows that semantic universe and mythical system are quasi-isomorphic. This is to say that the relations between the oppositions of a mythical system are structured by the relations among the states. A single type of relation—the mythical mediation—involves the functions. These remarks also apply to the symbolic system *mutatis mutandis*.

Narratives, Mythical System, and Sociolectal Semantic Universe

As Greimas suggests, a narrative manifests a micro-semantic universe that can be represented by a semiotic square. Because of the correspondence between semantic universe and mythical system discussed above, we must conclude that a narrative manifests in a privileged way two oppositions of macro-mythemes involving the most fundamental values presupposed by this narrative. This square is homologable with others manifested by other narratives (Lévi-Strauss's "variants" of the myth) and constitutes along with them a complete semantic universe. The structure by which the set of narratives of a given society inscribes its presupposed semantic universe (Greimas calls it the "sociolectal semantic universe") may be conceived of as a series of semiotic squares homologable with one another and thereby homologable with the fundamental semiotic square, which includes the opposition "life vs. death."[18] Thus, a society's set of narratives may be viewed, through a paradigmatic reading, as the metaphorical manifestations of the fundamental semiotic square characterizing the sociolectal semantic universe.

Therefore as soon as we have established the mythical system (the system of macro-mythemes) manifested through a set of narratives in a given society, it is possible to deduce from it the sociolectal semantic universe or presupposed system of axiologic values.[19] For this purpose we need to reduce the mythical system (which presents itself as a series of oppositions of complex terms) to a system of mythical states by bracketing out the functions. This system of states, which is the symbolic manifestation of a semantic universe, has for its structure a series of semiotic squares. By studying the relations that exist between the terms of each square it is then possible to bring to light the pertinent values of these terms over and beyond their symbolic manifestations.

This analytical process is the one represented in the first column of Figure 1. In actual practice this procedure will rarely be used, since it would require the simultaneous study of all the narratives of a given society. We will arrive at more rigorous results by elucidating the specific semantic universe of each narrative—which is a part of what Greimas terms the "idiolectal semantic universe." Then we can eventually consider how the various idiolectal semantic universes of these narratives combine to form a sociolectal semantic universe.

Narratives, Symbolic System, and Idiolectal Semantic Universe

The symbolic system presupposed by a particular narrative may be thought of in terms of the same model. By reading paradigmatically the set of symbolic elements (or mythemes) of this particular narrative—the symbolic system of this narrative—it may be viewed as the sum total of the metaphorical manifestations of the "fundamental" semiotic square underlying this narrative. Thus, the system formed by the states of a narrative's symbolic system may be thought of as a series of semiotic squares whose terms are the states of mythemes (and no longer those of macro-mythemes); it is the symbolic manifestation of what Greimas terms the "idiolectal semantic universe." These squares are homologable with one another and therefore homologable with a "fundamental" semiotic square, which also belongs to the mythical system in that its terms are also the states of macro-mythemes.[20] [Concrete examples are given on pp. 62 and 84.]

Once the narrative's symbolic system has been established, it is possible to deduce from it the idiolectal semantic universe presupposed by the narrative. We must first reduce the symbolic system to a system of states. By analyzing the relations that exist between the terms of each square, it then becomes possible to bring into focus the value of each term over and beyond its symbolic manifestation and, therefore, to elucidate the part of the idiolectal semantic universe the text presupposes.

In order for this final step of the analysis to occur, the symbolic system must already have been established in such a way that we may clearly identify the manifestations of the states of the mythemes. This is what the model of the relations between narrative system and symbolic system will enable us to do.

The analysis of each narrative also establishes one opposition of the mythical system (and thus one opposition of the sociolectal semantic universe). It is therefore possible to establish the mythical system by successively proceeding to the analysis of the various narratives rather than by using Lévi-Strauss's method. From this procedure we can expect more rigorous results, which could eventually be verified by means of Lévi-Strauss's criteria. Let us also note that a complex narrative may manifest several symbolic systems and that each system of values that corresponds to each of the symbolic systems seems to be what Greimas terms an isotopy.[21]

NARRATIVE SYSTEM, SYSTEM OF TRANSFORMATIONS, AND SYMBOLIC SYSTEM IN ELEMENTARY NARRATIVES

Although the narrative and symbolic systems are not isomorphic, they are nonetheless isotopic; certain elements of the one correspond to elements of the other, even though the structures that organize them into their respective systems are different. We can, therefore, ask this question: What are the narrative elements that correspond to the elements of the symbolic system? Or, more precisely, what are the narrative elements that, when projected upon the plane of the symbolic system, correspond to the state and function constituting the mytheme? Moreover, what are the narrative oppositions that would correspond to the oppositions of mythemes? In order to answer these questions we must first define the narrative system and its constitutive parts as formally as possible.[22]

In the present section we shall consider the case of "elementary narratives" that we could term single level narratives. They are complete narratives in their simplest form. In the next section we shall discuss the case of complex narratives—that is, narratives composed of several interrelated elementary narratives. Note that we have avoided the awkward repetition of the phrase "elementary narrative"; in the present section the noun "narrative" should be understood as referring to an elementary narrative.

Narrative Programs and Mythemes

The structure of an elementary narrative may be conceived of as a network of narrative programs.[23] Within this network we may distinguish two types of relations among the programs: the narrative hierarchy, which manifests the logic of the narrative development, and the narrative oppositions, which manifest the polemical dimension of the narrative. In order to examine these relations, it is useful to simplify the representation of the narrative programs by considering their minimal manifestation as a structure of exchange which Greimas[24] has shown to be a SUBJECT transferring an OBJECT to a RECEIVER. We may represent a program with the formula $S(O \rightarrow R)$; that is, read, a SUBJECT (S) transmits an OBJECT (O) to a RECEIVER (R). The formula $(O \rightarrow R)$ represents the performance of the narrative program which is the *transformation*—as

process—of the RECEIVER's state.[25]   All the other elements constituting
a narrative program are either qualifications of the SUBJECT (S) or
modalizations of the transformation $(O \rightarrow R)$.[26]   In this simplified formulation these qualifications and modalizations are presupposed, even though
they are not written down in order to clarify the notation.[27]

Such a formulation brings into view the possibility of establishing a
correspondence between narrative program and mytheme. In the narrative system the SUBJECT (S) and the transformation $(O \rightarrow R)$ both have
a *narrative meaning*—a referential-denotative meaning—which allows for
the integration of the program into a network of programs. When projected upon the plane of the symbolic system, the SUBJECT (S) and the
transformation $(O \rightarrow R)$ manifest two *symbolic values*—connotative
meanings—a state and a function, respectively. The symbolic value of
the SUBJECT is a "state" defined by all the qualifications of the SUB-
JECT, namely, by the investment of the actantial positions of the
HELPER (the vast majority of qualifications are manifestations of
HELPERS) and the SENDER (the investment of the actantial position of
the SENDER characterizes the SUBJECT's state in a fundamental way).
The place where the performance occurs is also a qualification of the
SUBJECT.[28]   The value of the performance $(O \rightarrow R)$, which is expressed
in the textual manifestation by a verb of action and its complements, is a
"function" in that it concerns the value of a transformation process. It
involves the interconnection of three elements: the value of the OBJECT
in circulation, the value of the RECEIVER (the qualifications of the
RECEIVER, i.e., his "state" before receiving the OBJECT), and the
modalization of the performance (for example, whether it is realized or
not).[29] [Examples of narrative programs are given on pp. 48ff.]

It seems, therefore, that the mytheme as a complex semantic unit may
correspond to the semantic value of a narrative program, which we can
establish by considering the symbolic values of the SUBJECT (the "state")
and of the transformation (the "function"). Yet for this to be true we
must show that the oppositions of the narrative programs *correspond* to
the oppositions of the mythemes.[30]

The Narrative Hierarchy (Level III)

The logic of the narrative development is the fundamental principle or-
ganizing the narrative system. In any elementary narrative we can identify
an ultimate program[31] toward the realization of which the whole narrative is
directed. The realization of this program is made possible by the fact that
a complete series of other programs—of subprograms—has taken place.

Based upon this observation, the narrative structure may be thought of as a *hierarchy of narrative programs*. In order for one program to take place the completion of a subprogram is required, and in order for the latter to have occurred the completion of a sub-subprogram is required, and so on. In other words, the SUBJECT (S^1) of an ultimate program[32] may communicate an OBJECT (O^1) to a RECEIVER (S^0) only if it has previously received the necessary HELPERS, that is to say if the SUBJECT (S^2) of a subprogram has communicated the modal-OBJECT (O^2) to (S^1), which in this program is in the actantial position of RECEIVER, and so forth. In a formal and greatly simplified fashion we may thus represent, as in Figure 5, the hierarchical succession of a program and its subprograms. In Figure 5, S^1 as the SUBJECT of the ultimate program

$$S^1(O^1 \rightarrow S^0)$$
$$\uparrow$$
$$S^2(O^2 \rightarrow S^1)$$
$$\uparrow$$
$$S^3(O^3 \rightarrow S^2)$$

etc.

Figure 5

can fulfill its program only because it has received a HELPER, O^2, which has been communicated to it as a result of the performance of a SUBJECT, S^2, which in turn was able to accomplish its program only because it had received a HELPER, O^3, which has been communicated by S^3, and so on.

However, the narrative manifestations are more complex than this. First, in numerous instances a SUBJECT will be able to accomplish its program only if several HELPERS have been attributed to it by means of several subprograms. To take an example, we could represent it as in Figure 6, where the OBJECTS Oa^2, Ob^2, and Oc^2 are all HELPERS that qualify S^1 as SUBJECT of his own program.

The narrative hierarchy of a long narrative will therefore be quite complex and will necessitate a representation in the form of a tree with multiple branches. A tree-representation is required even more to account for the *polemical* dimension of the narrative. In fact, up until now we have only considered the *principal* hierarchy, that is, the one which represents the logic of the narrative development leading to the conclusion of the narrative. The narrative's polemical dimension itself (which manifests the story of the OPPONENTS to the principal SUBJECTS) may be conceived of as a series of narrative programs with its own logic and, consequently, its own hierarchy. But, in fact, this polemical narrative is usually broken apart and its fragments interspersed within the principal narrative.[33] The polemical dimension juxtaposes the principal narrative programs with opposed narrative programs (eventually defined by certain of their sub-programs) that participate in the principal hierarchy because they justify

$$S^1(O^1 \rightarrow S^0)$$
$$\uparrow$$
$$Sa^2(Oa^2 \rightarrow S^1)$$
$$\uparrow$$
$$Sb^2(Ob^2 \rightarrow S^1)$$
$$\uparrow$$
$$Sc^2(Oc^2 \rightarrow S^1)$$
$$\uparrow$$
$$S^3(O^3 \rightarrow Sc^2)$$

Figure 6

the presence of certain subprograms. For example, a polemical narrative program may explain that the SUBJECT of a principal program might have need of certain HELPERS and that, as a result, a subprogram aiming toward the attribution of these HELPERS to the SUBJECT be introduced. The network of narrative programs may therefore be viewed as a single, though complex, hierarchy. [Consult pp. 45–48, 93.]

The Pertinent Transformations

Hierarchies of this sort are very detailed, due to the fact that they show all the narrative programs. We can imagine how many there are when we note that each verb of action manifests a program! It is now necessary to identify from among them those programs corresponding to the mythemes of the symbolic system, since these narrative programs are paired off in oppositions just like the mythemes. Thus, it is a matter of identifying the narrative oppositions without, however, assuming that they are to be fully identical with the oppositions of the symbolic system.

A narrative opposition is an opposition of narrative *processes*. Two programs are in *narrative* opposition when they manifest two "opposed" transformations, that is, two transformations which have opposite values. We are taking into consideration at the present moment not the opposi-tions that exist between the "states" of the SUBJECTS but only the oppositions between the "functions."

We can identify two opposed transformations in a formal way. First, the one must belong to the principal axis of the narrative hierarchy and the other to the polemical axis. Second, they are manifested either as the attribution of the same OBJECT to two opposed RECEIVERS,[34] $(O \rightarrow R)$ vs. $(O \rightarrow \bar{R})$, or as the attribution of two opposed OBJECTS to the same RECEIVER, $(O \rightarrow R)$ vs. $(\bar{O} \rightarrow R)$, or even as the attribution and nonattribution of the same OBJECT to the same RECEIVER, $(O \rightarrow R)$ vs. $(O \nrightarrow R)$.[35]

Certain of the narrative transformations—which we shall term *pertinent transformations*—are thus emphasized in the text by the very fact that they are contrasted with opposite transformations regardless of their respective places in the manifestation of the elementary narrative. All the other transformations must be considered secondary; they merely contribute to the semantic investment of the narrative programs manifesting the pertinent transformations.[36] Since the text pairs off the opposite transformations, we can expect that these narrative oppositions *correspond* to oppositions of mythemes. It is possible that the transformations correspond to the "functions." This is what we need to demonstrate.

The System of Pertinent Transformations (Level IV)

Following this identification of the pertinent transformations, we may then establish the system of narrative programs that manifests the pertinent transformations.[37] This system is structured by the network of relations that exists between the narrative transformations. Thus, the narrative transformations are organized according to the referential-denotative meanings of the narrative processes.[38] This system is manifested in the text by a series of oppositions of narrative programs. In each opposition one program is "principal" and the other "polemical," these two programs being characterized by opposite transformations. As a result the terms of these oppositions form two axes. On the one axis are inscribed the pertinent principal programs and on the other, the pertinent polemical programs. The hierarchical order of the *principal* programs will be respected in such a way that the axis of the pertinent principal programs becomes a simplified representation of the principal narrative hierarchy. On the polemical axis the pertinent programs are no longer in the order in which they were in the narrative hierarchy. They are now organized by opposition to the referential meaning of the transformations of the principal programs and no longer according to the needs of the narrative development structured by the hierarchy.[39]

A system of transformations may therefore be pictured as represented

in Figure 7. Note that $+P^1$, $+P^2$, $+P^3$, and $+P^4$ represent the series of
pertinent principal programs, while $-P^1$, $-P^2$, $-P^3$, and $-P^4$ represent
that of the pertinent polemical programs. The "$+$" and "$-$" signs, how-

$$(O^1 \rightarrow S^0) \;\; +P^1 \longleftrightarrow -P^1 \;\; (O^1 \rightarrow \overline{S}^0)$$

$$(O^2 \rightarrow S^1) \;\; +P^2 \longleftrightarrow -P^2 \;\; (\overline{O}^2 \rightarrow S^1)$$

$$(O^3 \rightarrow S^2) \;\; +P^3 \longleftrightarrow -P^3 \;\; (O^3 \nrightarrow S^2)$$

$$(O^1 \rightarrow S^3) \;\; +P^4 \longleftrightarrow -P^4 \;\; (O^4 \rightarrow \overline{S}^3)$$

Figure 7

ever, must not be read as "positive" and "negative" but as meaning
"principal" and "polemical" respectively.[40] The system depicted in Figure
7 is what we shall call, even though its constitutive elements are narrative
programs, the "system of pertinent transformations," because the structure of this system represents primarily the relations among the narrative
transformations. [A concrete example is given on pp. 52ff.]

System of Pertinent Transformations (Level IV) and Symbolic System (Level V)

A comparison of the system of pertinent transformations (essentially
narrative) with the symbolic system (which is structured by the relations
among states) will enable us to catch a glimpse of how the one is projected
upon the other. Let us first note the similarities between the two systems.

(1) There is in both instances a series of oppositions whose terms are
inscribed upon two axes: the one "principal" and the other "polemical"
in the case of the system of transformations, and the one "positive" and
the other "negative" in the case of the symbolic system.

(2) In both instances we have what amount to oppositions between
complex terms, not oppositions between semantic units that could be
entered onto semiotic squares.

When we consider their differences, we observe that:

(3) The complex terms are narrative programs in the first instance and
mythemes in the second. We have seen the possible correspondence between the symbolic value of the SUBJECT and the mythical state on the
one hand, and the narrative transformation and the mythical function on
the other.

(4) The oppositions are narrative oppositions in the one case and oppositions of symbolic values in the other. In the first instance the system of complex terms is structured by the network of relations existing among the "narrative transformations" which could correspond to the mythical functions. In the second instance these same complex terms are organized into a system by the network of relations existing among the static values possibly corresponding to the symbolic values manifested by the qualifications of the SUBJECTS.

(5) The axes of the system of transformations are defined narratively; the axis of the *principal* programs is opposed to that of the *polemical* programs. By contrast, the axes of the symbolic system are defined semantically; the axis of *positive* symbolic values is opposed to the axis of *negative* symbolic values. It could be that the axes of one system correspond to those of the other system.[41]

(6) The relations between two successive terms along the same axis are the relations of the "narrative logic" in the one case[42] and of semantic implication in the other.

These remarks enable us to anticipate that the system of transformations and the symbolic system are isotopic; the elements of the one appear, after projection, to correspond to the elements of the other. In order to establish this we must show that a constant rule for projecting elements in one plane onto another plane exists, thus permitting us to pass from one plane to another. We may do this by further considering the differences separating the two systems.

From the System of Pertinent Transformations (Level IV) to the Symbolic System (Level V)

Let us consider the passage from the system of transformations (which we can deduce from the narrative manifestation) to the symbolic system and, beyond it, to the semantic universe. This passage implies a progressive reduction of the narrative manifestation to a system of symbolic values. Within the system of transformations these values are present as constitutive elements of the narrative programs but are set in relation to one another by the intermediary of the narrative structure. Thus, in the system of transformations *the symbolic values are related narratively to each other*.

Take for example the symbolic values (manifested by the states) of the hero and the villain. They are placed in opposition within the system of transformations because their performances are opposite to one another.

But what are the relations between their symbolic values? As Greimas has shown, they are in a contradictory opposition.[43] In order for the hero and the villain to confront one another—in opposite performances—it is necessary that they be placed on the same (battle) ground and that their HELPERS be similar enough to allow for the confrontation to take place. Thus, although their symbolic values are opposed, they must belong to the same "world," to the same *isotopic space.* A contradictory opposition is in fact a partial opposition in the sense that it puts into play the semantic elements belonging to the same "world," which we term, following Greimas, an "isotopic space." For example, in a specific text both the hero and the villain might belong to the isotopic space "skillful fighter." The one manifests the assertion of "skillful" and the other the negation of "skillful"; for example, this hero is a *skillful* fighter and this villain is a *nonskillful* fighter. This example of the opposition of values of a hero and a villain is quite similar to the opposition "life" vs. "nonlife." Both terms belong to the isotopic space "life"; the former is the assertion of "life," the latter the negation of "life."

We may therefore say, following Greimas, that a *narrative opposition corresponds to an opposition of contradiction in a semiotic square of the symbolic system and of the semantic universe.* The validity of this claim is easily verifiable in the analysis of narrative texts. This statement expresses an extremely important characteristic of the projection of the system of transformations upon the symbolic system.

System of Transformations (Level IV), Symbolic System (Level V), and Semantic Universe (Level VII)

As we have seen above, a symbolic system is quasi-isomorphic with the semantic universe that it presupposes since it emphasizes the relations between states (or symbolic values that are manifested in the text by the qualifications of the SUBJECTS). The structure of the semantic universe may be represented by a series of homologable semiotic squares. The correspondence between this series of squares and the series of oppositions of the system of transformations can now be considered.

Before explaining this correspondence let us represent it graphically in Figure 8 by writing the oppositions of the narrative transformations in the preceding figure as contradictory oppositions of the squares of symbolic values without, however, changing the order of the terms of both axes. The states are represented as the values of the SUBJECTS.[44]

We propose to show that the symbolic system as well as the semantic universe can be obtained by making the polemical/negative axis of the system of transformations slide toward the top. Theoretically we might envision another possibility that must nevertheless be ruled out. If we make the polemical axis slide toward the bottom, this representation would imply that the progressive mediation represented by this succession of oppositions would find its resolution on the polemical axis. But this

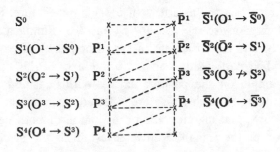

$$S^0 \qquad\qquad \bar{P}^1 \quad \bar{S}^1(O^1 \to \bar{S}^0)$$

$$S^1(O^1 \to S^0) \quad P^1 \qquad \bar{P}^2 \quad \bar{S}^2(\bar{O}^2 \to S^1)$$

$$S^2(O^2 \to S^1) \quad P^2 \qquad \bar{P}^3 \quad \bar{S}^3(O^3 \nrightarrow S^2)$$

$$S^3(O^3 \to S^2) \quad P^3 \qquad \bar{P}^4 \quad \bar{S}^4(O^4 \to \bar{S}^3)$$

$$S^4(O^4 \to S^3) \quad P^4$$

Figure 8

representation is contradicted by the fact that in the narrative the emphasis is placed upon the principal hierarchy. In Figure 8 the principal mytheme, P^4, is the mediating term of the final opposition ($P^3/\bar{P}^4$). Thus, the argument of the mythical logic reaches its completion along the axis that corresponds to the principal hierarchy.[45]

In order for this representation to be valid we must show that the states (or symbolic values of the SUBJECTS) form semiotic squares characterized by their three types of relations. Since some of the contradictory relations have already been established,[46] let us now consider in turn the relations of implication and of contrariety.[47]

In the system of transformations, the relations among the programs $+P^1$, $+P^2$, $+P^3$, . . . are relations of the logic of the narrative development; a certain transformation must take place in order for another to occur. But is it true that the relations between the symbolic values of the SUBJECTS S^1, S^2, S^3, . . . are those of implication? To show this, let us consider the typical investment of a succession of narrative programs in the principal narrative hierarchy represented above, in which the SUBJECT of a subprogram transmits a HELPER to the SUBJECT of the superior program. First, let us observe that both SUBJECTS belong in one way or another to the same semantic axis—to the positive axis in the theoretical example under consideration. Both SUBJECTS are indeed striving in their own way to bring about the same ultimate transformation and therefore are qualified in our theoretical examples as belonging to the set of "good" personages as opposed to the set of "evil" personages.

By confronting these SUBJECTS with other SUBJECTS belonging to the polemical dimension, the narrative selects from among the potential symbolic values of each narrative figure particular semantic features, which are pertinent because they are paired off into contradictory oppositions. Thus, if S^1 manifests the assertion of a semantic feature, $\overline{S}^1$ manifests its negation. It is likewise the case for S^2 and $\overline{S}^2$. Similarly, by having the SUBJECTS S^1 and S^2 participate in the principal hierarchy, the narrative makes clear their participation on one of the axes of the semantic universe —in our example on the positive axis. In this fashion other semantic features belonging to each figure are selected as pertinent features. The semantic features that manifest the participation of both personages along the same axis of the semantic universe establish the symbolic values of the SUBJECTS—their states—in a relation of implication. We may then say that the symbolic values of the SUBJECTS are in an anaphoric relation[48] in order to emphasize that a relation of partial semantic identity exists between two symbolic values belonging moreover to two different isotopic spaces. *The relation of implication is, therefore, the relation between two manifestations of a common semantic feature within two different isotopic spaces.* It is clear that this relationship exists among the symbolic values manifested by the SUBJECTS of two consecutive programs on one of the axes of the narrative hierarchy.

When we consider in more detail the relations between two of these manifestations it appears that the one (the anaphorizer) is "condensed"— expressing in a more specific and direct way the semantic feature that it holds in common with the other; and the other (the anaphorized) is in a state of extension—expressing in a less specific and direct way the same semantic trait. The higher a state in the narrative hierarchy, the more specific will be its manifestation of the axis. In this way S^2 is in a relationship of extension vis-à-vis S^1, and likewise S^3 is in a relationship of extension to S^2, and so on.[49]

The same argument applies to the relations between the transformations of the polemical axis:[50] $\overline{S}^2$ is in a state of extension vis-à-vis $\overline{S}^1$, and $\overline{S}^3$ in relation to $\overline{S}^2$, etc.

If we now consider one of the squares we can see that the relations $S^1/\overline{S}^2$ and $S^2/\overline{S}^3$ are, respectively, the oppositions of contraries and subcontraries. S^1 and $\overline{S}^2$ are the states that manifest in a "condensed" manner—as compared with those manifested by S^2 and $\overline{S}^3$—the semantic features that characterize the respective semantic axes. Since these axes are in a relation of contrariety, then S^1 and $\overline{S}^2$ are the contrary terms of the square. For similar reasons, S^2 and $\overline{S}^3$ are the subcontrary terms.

Thus the squares formed by making the polemical axis of the system of transformations slide upward are truly semiotic squares. The terms of these squares—the states or symbolic values—are complex semantic units that include at least two semantic features; one denotes their participation on an axis of the semantic universe, and the other their participation in an isotopic space.

NARRATIVE SYSTEM, SYSTEM OF TRANSFORMATIONS, AND SYMBOLIC SYSTEM IN COMPLEX NARRATIVES

The preceding model of the narrative structure applies to any elementary narrative. We now need to account for complex narratives, such as a Gospel or a novel.

A complex narrative can be viewed as a network of interwoven elementary narratives. How can we identify them formally? What are the laws that govern their interrelations? The answers to these questions will complement the above model and open up the possibility for defining a method of structural exegesis suited to the study of such complex narratives as the Gospels.

Formal Identification of the Elementary Narratives

We might be tempted to say that a complex narrative is composed of the stories of the various characters. Yet, as Vladimir Propp had already recognized, characters are not formal narrative units. An elementary narrative cannot be formally identified in terms of characters; it can be defined in terms of the formal characteristics that we have described above.

An elementary narrative can be formally viewed as a hierarchy of programs. The formal relation of these programs is represented above in Figures 5 and 6. A program, $S^1(O^1 \rightarrow S^0)$, can take place because in a preceding program, $S^2(O^2 \rightarrow S^1)$, an OBJECT/HELPER has been attributed to the SUBJECT of the first program. The interruptions of the formal pattern, $S^2(O^2 \rightarrow S^1) \rightarrow S^1(O^1 \rightarrow S^0)$, provide a rigorous criterion for isolating the elementary narratives within a complex narrative; these interruptions result from the introduction of an elementary narrative within another elementary narrative.

We must distinguish between three types of interruptions:

(1) *Interruptions of the formal pattern also manifesting breaks in the logical development of the story.* We see this in those events that take place concurrently with the original story and that are told even though they are not narratively related to it; for instance, in Mark 15:38 the reference to the curtain of the temple being torn in two. The juxtaposition of elementary narratives without narrative development from one to the other[51]—frequently found in the Gospel according to Mark—is another instance of the same phenomenon. Let us note that in these instances there is a second interruption of the formal narrative pattern and of the logical development of the story when the text comes back to the original story. These narrative units are therefore clearly isolated as *parallel narratives* (regardless of their length).

(2) *Interruptions of the formal pattern by an elementary narrative which, at first, breaks the narrative development though contributing to it.* We are referring here to the intersection of two narratives; one converges into the other. For instance, in Mark 15:6–15 we find the *converging narrative* of the crowd in relation to Pilate first interrupting and then merging into the narrative of Pilate and Jesus and contributing to its development.[52] We find another example in the story of Joseph of Arimathea, which intersects with the Pilate-soldiers story (Mark 15:42–47).

(3) *Interruptions of the formal pattern without interruption of the logic of the narrative development.* This occurs when the new narrative development is based upon an interpretation of the value of the preceding one.[53] For instance, in Mark 15:37 and 39 there is indeed a narrative development from Jesus' death on the cross to the centurion's confession. Yet, the formal pattern is interrupted; Jesus does not communicate any OBJECT/HELPER to the centurion (he is the SUBJECT of a quite different program, dying). The centurion's HELPER—that is, what allows him to utter his confession—is a knowledge of what has happened or, more specifically, an interpretative appropriation of these events.[54] In such a case we are in the presence of what we shall call a *diverging narrative,* which prolongs the primary narrative but at another narrative level. Let us emphasize that, although the diverging narratives are based upon the interpretative appropriation of the value of another narrative, their narrative developments may include a series of concrete (somatic) programs as well as a series of cognitive programs (such as those found in a dialogue).

We can, therefore, distinguish four types of elementary narratives within a complex one: the main narrative, the parallel narratives, the converging narratives, and the diverging narratives. It is possible to establish the narrative hierarchy of each of these elementary narratives by considering it in and of itself. Yet its principal and polemical axes are determined through their relations with the ultimate program of either the main narrative or its prolongation in the ultimate interpretative narrative.

The *parallel narratives* need to be analyzed completely on their own. The symbolic values that they presuppose must be read paradigmatically together with the symbolic values manifested by the parts of the main narrative or of diverging narratives with which they are juxtaposed in the narrative manifestation.

The *main, converging,* and *diverging narratives* are more closely inter-related because they all contribute in one way or another to the overall narrative development. However, at the semantic level we need to make a clear distinction between the main and converging narratives on the one hand and the diverging narratives on the other.

Converging narratives manifest primarily the stories of either HELPERS or OPPONENTS of SUBJECTS of the main narrative. As such they often manifest pertinent transformations that are opposed to those trans-formations manifested in the main narrative. Consequently, a main narra-tive and its converging narratives manifest a single system of pertinent transformations: *the system of pertinent transformations of the primary level.*

By contrast, the *diverging narratives* prolong the narrative development beyond this primary level. All the programs of diverging narratives are based upon the global interpretation of the value of at least a part of the narrative development of the primary level.[55] Because of these interpreta-tive presuppositions, these programs do not belong to the same semantic domain (to the same isotopy, as Greimas would say). In other words the diverging narratives should be analyzed separately from the primary-level narratives. Furthermore, when in a text we find diverging narratives based upon the interpretation of different parts of the primary-level narra-tive each of them must be analyzed separately[56] in accordance with the above model. Diverging narratives function as the main narrative does and therefore have their own converging narratives which participate in the interpretative level centered around a given diverging narrative.

In a complex narrative we shall find, therefore, on the one hand a sys-tem of pertinent transformations and a corresponding system of symbolic values at the primary level of the narrative, and on the other hand one or several such systems at the interpretative levels. The relation between a primary-level system of values and an interpretative-level system of values is similar to that of a mythical system and a symbolic system as described above (cf. Figure 2); the one is the detailed manifestation (in a micro-system of values) of the other. Yet, the detailed manifestation might be one or the other. At times the more fundamental values are found at the primary level; at other times, at the interpretative levels. In other words, while it is true that the more fundamental symbolic values are manifested at the end of an elementary narrative, it is not necessarily true that they are found at the end of a complex narrative because of the interrelation of the primary-level narrative with various diverging narratives. [Examples of elementary narratives are given on pp. 39ff.]

FROM MODEL TO METHOD

The model that we have just described expresses the relations between eight structural levels: the narrative manifestation as a network of elementary narratives, the elementary narrative, the narrative system (hierarchy of programs), the system of transformations, the symbolic system, the mythical system, the idiolectal semantic universe, and the sociolectal semantic universe. The precision of this model will permit us to derive from it an exegetical method that is well-defined and therefore relatively easy to use with the necessary rigor.

In order to elucidate the system of symbolic values—also termed semantic universe and system of convictions—presupposed by a narrative, the analysis needs to proceed in a step-by-step fashion from the textual manifestation to the semantic level.

Step 1. Identification of the elementary narratives and description of their interrelation as main narrative, converging narratives (altogether forming the primary level with the main narrative), diverging narratives (forming one or more interpretative levels), and parallel narratives. For this purpose the narrative development is carefully studied so as to show both the interruptions of the formal hierarchical pattern and the breaks in the logic of the narrative development. The parallel narratives are bracketed out (see Step 6). The other narrative units are then considered.

Step 2. Identification of the principal and polemical axes by means of the identification of the ultimate elementary narrative (which might belong either to the primary level or to an interpretative level) and within it the identification of the ultimate program. Except in the case where the text is concluded by a parallel narrative, the ultimate elementary narrative concludes the text.

(a) If the ultimate program[57] belongs to the primary level, it designates the principal narrative axis for the whole text. One can deduce the narrative axis to which the other programs belong in the primary level by studying their relations to this ultimate program. The narrative axes of the interpretative levels are deduced from their relations to the primary narrative level.

(b) If the ultimate program belongs to an interpretative level it only designates the principal narrative axis for this specific diverging narrative. One still needs to identify the ultimate program of the primary level. When this is done, one can proceed as above.

Step 3. Establishment of the system of pertinent transformations. Each level (the primary level and the several interpretative levels) *needs to be considered by itself.* In either case one proceeds in three stages:

(a) Identify the axis with the fewer programs. Accordingly, make a list of the principal or the polemical programs, writing them according to the formula S(O → R).

(b) Read the text over and identify the programs of the other axis manifesting functions[58] that are opposed to those of the programs in the previously established list.

(c) After eliminating the programs that are not pertinent (i.e., those that do not have an opposite), write the system of pertinent transformations according to Figure 7. To do this, it is necessary to organize the *principal* programs so that they are in the order of the narrative development (the development progressing from the bottom toward the top of the diagram).[59]

Step 4. Establishment of the symbolic system. As noted above, it is easy to transform the system of pertinent transformations of an elementary narrative and its converging narratives into its symbolic system. It is a little more difficult in the case of a complex narrative because of the interrelation of the various narrative levels. To avoid errors we need to proceed in two stages:

(a) Diagram the interrelation of the various systems of transformations following the model of Figure 2, so that the systems of the interpretative levels form branches moving out of the system of the primary level. Be sure that the "branches" are attached to the program they interpret (be it on the principal or the polemical axis).[60]

(b) Slide all the polemical axes upward so as to have the SUBJECTS of opposite programs in a contradictory relation in the newly formed semiotic squares. Since some principal programs will participate in both the squares of the primary level and in squares of secondary level(s), their opposite programs (which will be their contradictory in each case) will need to "go up in the branches" as well as remain on the primary level.

Step 5. Study of the semantic universe.

(a) Disregarding the functions, consider now the narrative manifestation of the symbolic values of the SUBJECT. Going back to the text, identify the specific qualifications of the SUBJECT of each program: its various HELPERS (be they concrete objects, locations, temporal notations, some type of knowledge or feeling), its OPPONENTS, and its SENDER.

(b) Study in each square the three types of relations in order to identify the pertinent semantic features that compose the symbolic values.

Step 6.   Study of the parallel narratives. Once the semantic universe presupposed by the primary and secondary levels has been established, the parallel narratives (if there are any) can be studied. The long parallel narratives need to be analyzed as any other elementary narrative (Steps 2 to 5 above). The relations between the symbolic systems of the parallel narratives and the symbolic systems of the other elementary narratives can then be studied.

3

Structural Exegesis of
Mark 15 and 16

Our exegesis of Mark 15 and 16 aims at elucidating the semantic universe (or system of symbolic values) that is presupposed by this text and that characterizes the faith of its author (or redactor). We shall follow the method outlined in the concluding part of the preceding chapter. We have selected the last chapters of the Gospel because a study of the end of a text allows the exegete to identify without ambiguity the ultimate program of the text and therefore its narrative axes (the principal and polemical axes). We shall consider the short ending of the Gospel (ending in 16:8), which has been designated as the original text by traditional exegesis.[1] A twofold break, that is a break both in the formal narrative pattern of the hierarchy and in the narrative development, isolates chapters 15 and 16 from the end of chapter 14 (14:72). Mark 15 and 16 can therefore be viewed as a narrative unit that can be analyzed independently of the rest of the Gospel.[2]

IDENTIFICATION OF THE ELEMENTARY NARRATIVES

The first stage of our exegesis aims at the identification of the primary narrative level and of the interpretative narrative levels manifested by the text. Since the primary level can be expected to form the core of the narrative, our main concern will be to identify with great care the diverging narratives (which form the interpretative narrative levels) and the parallel narratives. The converging narratives are merely a part of the primary narrative level and thus are to be analyzed along with the main narrative. In a first reading we shall take note of the breaks in the formal hierarchical pattern and in the logic of the narrative development, and in so doing we shall set aside the diverging and parallel narratives.

Mark 15:1–15

[1]And as soon as it was morning the chief priests, with the elders and scribes, and the whole council held a consultation; and they bound Jesus and led him away and delivered him to Pilate. [2]And Pilate asked him, "Are you the King of the Jews?" And he answered him, "You have said so." [3]And the chief priests accused him of many things. [4]And Pilate again asked him, "Have you no answer to make? See how many charges they bring against you." [5]But Jesus made no further answer, so that Pilate wondered.

[6]Now at the feast he used to release for them one prisoner whom they asked. [7]And among the rebels in prison, who had committed murder in the insurrection, there was a man called Barabbas. [8]And the crowd came up and began to ask Pilate to do as he was wont to do for them. [9]And he answered them, "Do you want me to release for you the King of the Jews?" [10]For he perceived that it was out of envy that the chief priests had delivered him up. [11]But the chief priests stirred up the crowd to have him release for them Barabbas instead. [12]And Pilate again said to them, "Then what shall I do with the man whom you call the King of the Jews?" [13]And they cried out again, "Crucify him." [14]And Pilate said to them, "Why, what evil has he done?" But they shouted all the more, "Crucify him." [15]So Pilate, wishing to satisfy the crowd, released for them Barabbas; and having scourged Jesus, he delivered him to be crucified.

In these verses we notice a number of twofold breaks (i.e., breaks both in the formal hierarchical pattern and in the narrative development) which manifest either the presence of converging narratives or that of parallel narratives. In Mark 15:1–15 each of these breaks manifests the presence of a converging narrative.

Verse 6 is a narrative about Pilate's usual actions in the past (what he used to do at the feast).

Verse 7 is a narrative about Barabbas.

Verse 8 is a narrative about the crowd merging into the narrative of verse 6 then with the main narrative.

Verse 11 is a narrative about the chief priests stirring up the crowd, which merges into the main narrative (in which the crowd is now included).

These short converging narratives belong to the primary narrative level. They provide "background" information about some of the characters of the main narrative.

Mark 15:16–20

[16]And the soldiers led him away inside the palace (that is, the praetorium); and they called together the whole battalion. [17]And they clothed him in a purple cloak, and plaiting a crown of thorns they put it on him. [18]And they began to salute him, "Hail, King of the Jews!" [19]And they

struck his head with a reed, and spat upon him, and they knelt down in homage to him. [20]And when they had mocked him, they stripped him of the purple cloak, and put his own clothes on him. And they led him out to crucify him.

These verses prolong the narrative development without break.[3] Thus, they belong to the main narrative, except for the phrase "that is, the praetorium" (v. 16b). This parenthetical note given by the enunciator can be viewed as belonging to a specific diverging narrative, the narrative about the relations of the enunciator (the author as manifested in the narrative) and his "enunciatees" (the readers as manifested in the narrative). The note is based upon the interpretation of a specific element of the main narrative: the phrase "inside the palace" is perceived by the enunciator as not being specific enough for his readers.

Mark 15:21–33

[11]And they compelled a passer-by, Simon of Cyrene, who was coming in from the country, the father of Alexander and Rufus, to carry his cross. [22]And they brought him to the place called Golgotha (which means the place of a skull). [23]And they offered him wine mingled with myrrh; but he did not take it. [24]And they crucified him, and divided his garments among them, casting lots for them, to decide what each should take. [25]And it was the third hour, when they crucified him. [26]And the inscription of the charge against him read, "The King of the Jews." [27]And with him they crucified two robbers, one on his right and one on his left. [28]. . . [29]And those who passed by derided him, wagging their heads, and saying, "Aha! You who would destroy the temple and build it in three days, [30]save yourself, and come down from the cross!" [31]So also the chief priests mocked him to one another with the scribes, saying, "He saved others; he cannot save himself. [32]Let the Christ, the King of Israel, come down now from the cross, that we may see and believe." Those who were crucified with him also reviled him.

[33]And when the sixth hour had come, there was darkness over the whole land until the ninth hour.

These verses prolong the preceding narrative development, and thus they prolong the main narrative. Yet they include several breaks.

Verse 21 is a short converging narrative about Simon of Cyrene.

Verse 22b, "which means the place of a skull," manifests another part of the diverging narrative concerning the enunciator and his "enunciatees."

Verse 27 is the first part of a narrative about the robbers who have been crucified with Jesus. The second part is found in verse 32. We shall come back to this.[4]

Verses 29 and 30 manifest a break in the formal hierarchical pattern (none of the personages of the preceding narrative development transmit anything to the passersby so as to give them the possibility of insulting Jesus), yet the logic of the narrative development is not interrupted (it is because Jesus has been crucified that they can insult him as they do). We have noted above that in such a case we are dealing with a diverging narrative. Indeed, the action of the passersby presupposes an interpretation of the value of the events described in the preceding verses, the crucifixion of Jesus by the soldiers. Furthermore, the interpretative process is manifested[5] by the phrase "wagging their heads." Thus the diverging narrative about the passersby belongs to an interpretative narrative level. The content of the mocking ("Aha! You who would destroy the temple and build it in three days, save yourself, and come down from the cross!") refers to still another part of the main narrative, what Jesus has said according the false witnesses (14:58). Thus, the diverging narrative is based upon an interpretation of "the crucified one who has made such a proclamation."

Verse 31 and the first part of verse 32 manifest a twofold diverging narrative. "The chief priests mocked him to one another with the scribes, saying" (v. 31a) is a diverging narrative that is similar to the preceding one. In addition, the content of this mocking includes a hypothetical main narrative (Jesus who has saved others should come down from the cross) prolonged by a hypothetical diverging narrative that is based upon its interpretation. The interpretative process is manifested by the verb "seeing." The hypothetical performance that would follow is the act of believing in Jesus as Christ, King of Israel. These two diverging narratives are closely interrelated and belong to the same interpretative level. Both are based upon the interpretation of the event "Jesus crucified." Yet the second makes it clear that what is interpreted is not merely the crucifixion process but also the expected end result of the crucifixion (either the hypothetical end result, Jesus coming down from the cross, or the actual end result, Jesus dying on the cross).

The end of verse 32, the insults of those who were crucified with Jesus, is another diverging narrative, to which verse 27 also belongs. It is also based upon the interpretation of the event "Jesus crucified."

Verse 33 is isolated by two twofold breaks (one of them separating it from verse 32, the other from verse 34). It is a parallel narrative that is quite elliptic.

Mark 15:34–46

[34]And at the ninth hour Jesus cried with a loud voice, "Eloi, Eloi lama sabachthani?" which means, "My God, my God, why hast thou forsaken me?" [35]And some of the bystanders hearing it said, "Behold, he is calling

Elijah." [36]And one ran and, filling a sponge full of vinegar, put it on a reed and gave it to him to drink, saying, "Wait, let us see whether Elijah will come to take him down." [37]And Jesus uttered a loud cry, and breathed his last. [38]And the curtain of the temple was torn in two, from top to bottom. [39]And when the centurion, who stood facing him, saw that he thus breathed his last, he said, "Truly this man was the Son of God!"

[40]There were also women looking on from afar, among whom were Mary Magdalene, and Mary the mother of James the younger and of Joses, and Salome, [41]who, when he was in Galilee, followed him, and ministered to him; and also many other women who came up with him to Jerusalem.

[42]And when evening had come, since it was the day of Preparation, that is, the day before the sabbath, [43]Joseph of Arimathea, a respected member of the council, who was also himself looking for the kingdom of God, took courage and went to Pilate, and asked for the body of Jesus. [44]And Pilate wondered if he were already dead; and summoning the centurion, he asked him whether he was already dead. [45]And when he learned from the centurion that he was dead, he granted the body to Joseph. [46]And he bought a linen shroud, and taking him down, wrapped him in the linen shroud, and laid him in a tomb which had been hewn out of the rock; and he rolled a stone against the door of the tomb.

With verse 34 the text comes back to the main narrative: Jesus cried out because he has been crucified. Two diverging narratives are based upon the interpretation of Jesus' cry.

The second part of verse 34 manifests a diverging narrative of the enunciator, who provides an interpretation of Jesus' words.

Verses 35 and 36 manifest a second diverging narrative based upon another interpretation of Jesus' words.

Verse 37 (Jesus expiring) belongs to the main narrative.

Verse 38 (the curtain of the temple torn in two) is an elliptic parallel narrative.

Verse 39 (the centurion's confession) is a first diverging narrative based upon an interpretation ("seeing") of the way Jesus died ("[he] saw that he *thus* breathed his last").

Verses 40 and 41 (about the women) form another diverging narrative based upon an interpretation (they were looking) of Jesus' death, which is not yet fully developed (it will be later on). These verses include a converging narrative merging into a diverging narrative, the narrative about what the women did earlier.

With verses 42 and 43, we find a new twofold break: these verses manifest the converging narrative about Joseph of Arimathea merging into the narrative about Pilate and the centurion (vv. 44–46), which prolongs the main narrative and therefore belongs to it.

Mark 15:47—16:8

⁴⁷Mary Magdalene and Mary the mother of Joses saw where he was laid.
¹⁶˸¹And when the sabbath was past, Mary Magdalene, and Mary the mother of James, and Salome, bought spices, so that they might go and anoint him. ²And very early on the first day of the week they went to the tomb when the sun had risen. ³And they were saying to one another, "Who will roll away the stone for us from the door of the tomb?" ⁴And looking up, they saw that the stone was rolled back—it was very large. ⁵And entering the tomb, they saw a young man sitting on the right side, dressed in a white robe; and they were amazed. ⁶And he said to them, "Do not be amazed; you seek Jesus of Nazareth, who was crucified. He has risen, he is not here; see the place where they laid him. ⁷But go, tell his disciples and Peter that he is going before you to Galilee; there you will see him, as he told you." ⁸And they went out and fled from the tomb; for trembling and astonishment had come upon them; and they said nothing to any one, for they were afraid.

Verse 15:47 introduces a new diverging narrative (it manifests a break in the formal hierarchical pattern without interrupting the logic of the narrative development), which is based upon an interpretation of the burial of Jesus by Joseph of Arimathea. This diverging narrative unfolds itself without interruption up to 16:5 ("entering the tomb").

With the second part of verse 16:5 there begins a secondary diverging narrative which is based upon an interpretation of the end of the preceding diverging narrative (15:47—16:5a). The performance "being amazed" (or afraid) breaks the formal hierarchical pattern without interrupting the logic of the narrative development. If the women are struck by fear it is not because the tomb or the young man have communicated to them a helper (whatever it might be) but because they have interpreted ("seeing") in a specific way their own presence in the tomb.

Verses 6 and 7 manifest another secondary diverging narrative based upon another interpretation (by the young man) of the women's presence in the tomb. The end of verse 8 ("and they said nothing to any one for they were afraid") is the conclusion of this diverging narrative and thus belongs to it.

The first part of verse 8 ("They went out and fled from the tomb") prolongs the primary diverging narrative: after entering the tomb, they go out from it.

The interrelation of the elementary narratives in the complex narrative Mark 15:1—16:8 can now be represented as in Table 1. The discussion concerning the identification of the narrative axes has been anticipated in this table. The symbols (+) and (−) mark the narrative axis (either principal or polemical) to which the diverging elementary narratives and various segments of the main narrative predominantly belong (even though they might include narrative programs belonging to the other axis).

IDENTIFICATION OF THE NARRATIVE AXES

At the end of the text we find a secondary diverging narrative: the young man's speech should be prolonged (but is not) by the women's communication of the message about the resurrection to the disciples. This is the ultimate narrative. This speech manifests almost exclusively the principal narrative axis.[6] The women's fear (another secondary diverging narrative), which is opposed to the preceding narrative, belongs to the polemical axis. Consequently, the women running away (primary diverging narrative) manifest the polemical axis, and the women coming to the tomb (a movement that is necessary for an eventual communication of the message) manifest predominantly the principal axis. We shall term these narratives Interpretative Level I.[7]

The main narrative (which ends with Joseph of Arimathea burying Jesus) shows a triple ultimate program with Joseph as SUBJECT: closing the tomb with a stone; laying Jesus in the tomb; wrapping Jesus in the shroud. By definition, this triple program belongs to the principal narrative axis. Joseph performs it after overcoming Pilate's objections. In verses 44–46 most of the programs which have Pilate as SUBJECT belong to the polemical axis to the extent that they express Pilate's resistance to Joseph's request (Pilate wants to be sure Jesus is actually dead). Consequently all the programs that bring about Jesus' death belong themselves to the polemical axis of the main narrative. Thus the part of the main narrative found in 15:1–46 is predominantly polemical.[8] Generally speaking, this observation also applies to the converging narratives related to this part of the main narrative, yet a detailed study is necessary before each can be said to belong to either of the two axes.

Each of the diverging narratives found in 15:1–46 manifests one axis (either the principal or the polemical). They are therefore opposed to each other in the form of principal diverging narratives versus polemical diverging narratives (according to the type of interpretation upon which they are based). Thus, in the case of the two diverging narratives that interpret Jesus' cry, the enunciator's interpretation (15:34b) is posited as true while the interpretation proposed by the people thinking that he is calling upon Elijah (15:35–36) is posited as false. Therefore, the first diverg-

TABLE 1

PRIMARY NARRATIVE LEVEL		INTERPRETATIVE NARRATIVE LEVELS		PARALLEL NARRATIVES
Converging Narratives	*Main Narrative*	*Diverging Narratives*	*Secondary Diverging Narratives*	
		(−) women running away (16:8a)	(+) young man's speech (16:6–7, 8b)	
			(−) the women's fear (16:5b)	
		(+) women at the tomb (15:47–16:5a)		
Joseph of Arimathea (15:42–43)	(+) Pilate, centurion, and Joseph: burial (15:44–46)	(+) women at Golgotha (15:40–41)		curtain of the temple (15:38)
		(+) centurion's confession (15:39)		
	(−) Jesus' death (15:37)			
		(−) people expecting Elijah's coming (15:35–36)		
	(+) Jesus' cry (15:34a)	(+) enunciator's interpretation (15:34b)		darkness (15:33)

(15:27, 32c)

[Jesus coming down from the cross: hypothetical] (15:32a)

(–) hypothetical faith of chief priests and scribes (15:32b)

(–) insults by chief priests and scribes (15:31–32a)

(–) insults by passersby (15:29–30)

(+) enunciator, place of a skull (15:22b)

(–) soldiers and Jesus, crucifixion (15:21–26)

(+) enunciator, praetorium (15:16b)

(–) soldiers and Jesus in the palace (15:16–20)

Simon of Cyrene (15:21)

(–) Pilate, Jesus, chief priests, crowd, Barabbas (15:6–15)

chief priests and crowd (15:11)

crowd (15:8); Barabbas (15:7)

What Pilate used to do (15:6)

(–) chief priests, Jesus, and Pilate (15:1–5)

47

ing narrative is principal and the second is polemical. These two diverging narratives form what we shall term Interpretative Level III.

The diverging narratives that express the mocking of Jesus by the passersby (15:29–30), by the chief priests (15:31–32a, b), and by the robbers (15:27, 32c) are clearly polemical. As noted above, they interpret both the "crucified Jesus" and the expected end result of the crucifixion. The centurion's confession (15:39), which interprets in an opposite way the actual end result of the crucifixion, is therefore a diverging narrative belonging to the principal axis. Similarly, the diverging narrative of the women at Golgotha (15:40–41) belongs to the principal axis since it is based upon the interpretation of the actual crucifixion. Note that it also involves the interpretation of certain events in Jesus' ministry just as the opposite diverging narratives about the passersby and the chief priests do. All these diverging narratives form what we shall term Interpretative Level II.

THE SYSTEM OF PERTINENT TRANSFORMATIONS

The System of Pertinent Transformations of the Primary Narrative Level

In order to elucidate the system of pertinent transformations of the primary narrative level (the main narrative and its converging narratives), we first need to determine which axis has the smaller number of narrative programs. In the present case it is the principal axis. Our next task is to establish a list of the transformations that belong to the shorter axis by using the formula $S(O \to R)$ or $S(O \to S)$. Thus, in the present case we need to study the "actions" (the predicates of the category of "doing") of the principal axis. The qualifications (the predicates of the category of "being/having") will be studied later on.[9] The programs that belong to the principal axis are those that have the same aim as the ultimate program. In order to identify them it is convenient to read the text "upside down," starting with the end of the primary level (its ultimate program) and progressing toward its beginning.

Rather than describe this process in detail, we will provide a list of the narrative programs that belong to the principal axis of Mark 15:42–46 and follow it by explanatory remarks.

NARRATIVE PROGRAMS OF THE PRINCIPAL AXIS IN MARK 15:42–46

Narrative Manifestations	*Narrative Programs* (NP)
46e: he rolled a stone against the door of the tomb	NP 46e: Joseph (stone → door of the tomb)
46d: (he) laid him in a tomb	NP 46d: Joseph (Jesus → tomb)

Narrative Manifestations	*Narrative Programs* (NP)
46c: (he) wrapped him with the linen shroud	NP 46c: Joseph (shroud → Jesus)
46b: taking him down (from the cross)	NP 46b: Joseph (non-cross → Jesus)
46a: he bought a linen shroud	NP 46a: Joseph (shroud → Joseph)
45c: granted him the body (and 46b²)	NP 45c, 46b²: Joseph (body of Jesus → Joseph)
45b: he granted him	NP 45b: Pilate (permission → Joseph)
45a: he learned from the centurion	NP 45a: centurion (message → Pilate)
43c: asked for the body of Jesus	NP 43c: Joseph (mandate → Pilate)
43b: went to Pilate	NP 43b: Joseph (Pilate → Joseph)
43a: (Joseph arriving)	NP 43a: Joseph (unspecified place → Joseph)

Remarks:

NP 46e: "Rolling a stone against the door of the tomb" is the attribution of "stone" (OBJECT) to the "door of the tomb" (RECEIVER) . . . or vice versa. A transformation indeed results in the conjunction of an OBJECT and a RECEIVER, but it is often difficult to discern which is which. In practice, the RECEIVER can be recognized because it is the actant that later becomes the SUBJECT of another program. Since neither the stone nor the tomb becomes the SUBJECT of a program, they are arbitrarily designated as OBJECT and RECEIVER. We will need to keep in mind that the opposite designation is also possible when looking for the polemical transformations corresponding to the principal transformations.

NP 46d and NP 46c: The preceding remark also applies here.

NP 46a: This formulation only represents the transformation manifested by the action of "buying." Buying is the attribution of something (OBJECT) to oneself (RECEIVER) by means of specific HELPERS (a seller, the society, money, etc.).

NP 45c and NP 45b: "Granting the body" involves two transformations, as can be seen if we translate this phrase "giving him the permission to take the body." "Taking the body" is what Joseph does when bringing Jesus down from the cross (NP 46b).

(Verse 44 is polemical, since it manifests Pilate's objection to Joseph's request. Thus it does not belong to the list of principal programs.)

NP 43c: Asking something of someone is giving a "mandate" (OBJECT) to someone (RECEIVER). The content of the mandate is another program, which at this point is merely manifested as a contractual statement

(CS 1) that is not yet accepted (or rejected). In the present case this second program is NP 45b, followed by NP 45c, 46b[2].

NP 43b: To avoid omitting any pertinent program, we shall record all the movements as if they were independent programs. It is indeed difficult to know at first glance if the text simply manifests a disjunction/conjunction statement (DS, which is a part of a program) or if it manifests a program of movement that may be a pertinent program. In fact, a DS is merely a program of movement that is not pertinent.

NP 43a: The arrival of Joseph is expressed in the Greek text by ἐλθὼν Ἰωσήφ (it is omitted in the RSV).

A graphic representation of the complete narrative hierarchy can be made to ensure that no program is omitted. This has been prepared for the whole text in order to control our analysis. Yet we have chosen not to present it for reasons of space; in addition to the fourteen pages of diagrams, we would have had to provide a long explanation of it. We provide an example of such a narrative hierarchy in an Appendix to the present chapter (p. 93).

The programs identified as belonging to the principal axis in the verses studied above manifest a respectful attitude toward Jesus (we shall be more precise below). The programs that express the abuses against Jesus are therefore polemical. All the programs that, directly or indirectly, bring about Jesus' death belong to the polemical axis. Therefore, the rest of the main narrative is primarily polemical, although it includes a number of principal programs.

NARRATIVE PROGRAMS OF THE PRINCIPAL AXIS IN MARK 15:1–37

Narrative Manifestations	*Narrative Programs* (NP)
34a: Jesus cried with a loud voice "Eloi . . ."	NP 34a: Jesus (Aramaic message → X)
21c: a passerby, Simon of Cyrene, who was coming in from the country	NP 21c: Simon (undefined location → Simon)
14b: what evil has he done?	NP 14b: crowd (justification of accusation → Pilate)
14a: Pilate said to them (what evil has he done?)	NP 14a: Pilate (mandate → crowd)
10a: he perceived that it was out of envy that the chief priests (had delivered him up)	NP 10a: Pilate (knowledge about the envy of the chief priests → Pilate)

Narrative Manifestations	Narrative Programs (NP)
9c: me to release for you the King of the Jews	NP 9c: Pilate (King of the Jews → crowd)
9b: Do you want?	NP 9b: crowd (mandate → Pilate)
9a: And he (Pilate) answered them	NP 9a: Pilate (mandate → crowd)
8c: Pilate to do as he was wont to do for them (the crowd)	NP 8c: Pilate ([prisoner] → crowd)
8b: (the crowd) began to ask Pilate (also 6b)	NP 8b: crowd (mandate → Pilate)
8a: The crowd came up (to Pilate)	NP 8a: crowd (Pilate → crowd)
6a: at the feast he used to release for them one prisoner	NP 6a: Pilate (prisoner → crowd)
5b: so that Pilate wondered	NP 5b: Jesus (astonishment → Pilate)
5a: But Jesus made no further answer (also 4b, "have you no answer to make")	NP 5a: Jesus (non-response to accusation → Pilate)
2c: "You have said so" (that I am the King of the Jews)	NP 2c: Pilate (title: King of the Jews → Jesus)
2b: Jesus answered him	NP 2b: Jesus (message → Pilate)

Remarks:

NP 34a: This cry is not merely the consequence of the crucifixion (as in the case of the cry in verse 37); it manifests Jesus' resistance to his opponents. This is the reason this narrative program belongs to the principal axis (while verse 37 belongs to the polemical axis).

NP 21c: Simon's movement does not belong to the polemical axis since in itself it does not contribute to Jesus' crucifixion. Rather, it is his being "compelled" by the soldiers (a collective polemical SUBJECT) to carry the cross that is polemical.

NP 14a and NP 14b: This question manifests Pilate's opposition to the crucifixion. Asking a question is giving a mandate to somebody, the mandate to give some type of information. This mandate establishes another program, which also belongs to the principal axis (NP 14b). This program does not unfold (the mandate is not accepted by the crowd and consequently the program is interrupted at its first contractual statement, CS 1). In order to avoid any omission, we must register this program on the principal axis, despite the fact that it is not carried out. It may still be pertinent if it is opposed to a fulfilled polemical program (actually the analysis will show that there is no such polemical program, but we cannot exclude this possibility at the outset).

NP 10a: He "perceived," that is, he attributed to himself a cognitive OBJECT: the knowledge about the envy of the chief priests.

NP 9a and NP 9b: Through his question Pilate asks (he gives a mandate to the crowd, NP 9a) that the crowd give him a mandate (NP 9b).

NP 8a, NP 8b, NP 8c: The various elements of this verse belong to the principal axis: the crowd becomes OPPONENT to Jesus after having been stirred up by the chief priests.

NP 6a: Pilate's habitual action appears here as a means for saving Jesus from crucifixion.

NP 2b, NP 2c, NP 5a, NP 5b: Jesus' attitude has made Pilate into a temporary ally. Thus these four programs belong to the principal axis. The formulation of these programs does not present any difficulty except in the cases of NP 5b and NP 5a. The narrative transformation of NP 5b is clear: the OBJECT is "astonishment"; the RECEIVER is "Pilate." But who is the SUBJECT? It is "Jesus' non-answer to Pilate," which we have represented with the term "Jesus." It could also be represented by the term "Pilate," which should then be read as "Pilate as qualified by Jesus' attitude." This should be a reminder that at this point in the analysis we are involved in identifying the narrative transformations. The SUBJECTS and their qualifications will be considered in detail in the context of our study of the symbolic system. Thus, at this stage of the analysis the terms designating the SUBJECTS should be viewed simply as a first, descriptive approximation of a complex symbolic manifestation.

NP 5a could be represented as an interrupted program (i.e., an interrupted transformation): Jesus (response to accusations $\nrightarrow$ Pilate). Yet this "non-response" brings about Pilate's astonishment; it transforms Pilate's state. This is why it is better to represent it as a transformation with a negative OBJECT: Jesus (non-response to accusations $\rightarrow$ Pilate).

The System of Pertinent Transformations
of the Primary Level

We have identified as carefully as possible all the narrative programs along the principal axis of the primary level, including those that are not realized (manifesting, in this case, potential transformations). It remains for us to show which among them are pertinent in that they manifest transformations that are opposed to those of the polemical programs. For this purpose we need to read over the text of the primary level in order to compare systematically each polemical narrative program with the list established above. Proceeding in this way,[10] we obtain the following system of pertinent transformations:

*NP 46c Joseph (shroud → Jesus)	NP 17a soldiers (purple cloak → Jesus)
*NP 46b Joseph (non-cross → Jesus)	NP 24a, soldiers (state of crucified 25 → Jesus)
*NP 45b Pilate (permission → Joseph)	NP 15a Pilate (satisfaction → crowd)
*NP 43e Joseph (mandate → Pilate)	NP 13a crowd (mandate → Pilate)
NP 34a Jesus (Aramaic message → X)	*NP 37a Jesus (cry → X)
NP 9c Pilate (King of the Jews → crowd)	*NP 15b Pilate (Barabbas → crowd)
NP 5b Jesus (astonishment → Pilate)	*NP 14c crowd (mandate → Pilate)
NP 4b, Jesus (non-response to 5a accusation → Pilate)	*NP 14b crowd (non-justification of accusation → Pilate)
NP 9a Pilate (mandate → crowd)	*NP 11a chief priests (excitement → crowd)[11]

All the other transformations—whether they belong to the principal axis or to the polemical axis—are "non-pertinent." We could not locate any transformations opposite to them at the primary narrative level of our text.

NP 46c vs. *NP 17a:* In both cases the RECEIVER is "Jesus."[12] The OBJECTS "shroud" (or linen shroud) and "purple cloak" (or purple linen) are formally opposed by the fact that they are two pieces of cloth of different types and usages. The two functions are also different; one is a gesture of respect while the other is a mocking gesture. Yet this last statement expresses not the narrative opposition but the semantic opposition manifested by qualifications of the two SUBJECTS.

NP 46b vs. *NP 24a, 25:* In both cases "Jesus" is the RECEIVER. The OBJECTS, "non-cross" (state of being non-crucified) and "cross" (state of being crucified), are opposed to each other.

NP 45b vs. *NP 15a:* The RECEIVERS, "Joseph" (Jesus' disciple since he was looking for the kingdom of God) and the "crowd" (Jesus' OPPO-

NENT at this point of the narrative), are different and opposed to each other. The OBJECTS can be equated: a "permission" is a "satisfaction."

NP 43e vs. *NP 13a:* In both cases the same RECEIVER, Pilate, receives a mandate. These two mandates are opposed to each other. The one (NP 43e) is given by Joseph in order to obtain Jesus' body so as to bring him down from the cross (to "uncrucify" him) and to bury him; the other (NP 13a) is given by the crowd with the result that Pilate crucifies Jesus.

NP 34a vs. *NP 37a:* In both cases the RECEIVERS are undefined; they can therefore be equated with each other. The OBJECTS are opposed to each other: in one case it is a *message* (an articulate discourse, even though it is in Aramaic), in the other it is an inarticulate *cry*.

NP 9c vs. *NP 15b:* The "crowd" is the RECEIVER in each of the two programs. The OBJECTS, "King of the Jews" (neither rebel nor murderer) and "Barabbas" (rebel and murderer), are opposed to each other.

NP 5b vs. *NP 14c:* In both cases "Pilate" is the RECEIVER. The OBJECTS are opposed to each other: on the one hand, a mandate given by the crowd demands that Pilate become an opponent to Jesus; on the other hand, the astonishment given to Pilate by Jesus' silence functions as a mandate demanding that Pilate take a positive attitude toward Jesus and defend him.

NP 4b vs. *NP 14b:* In both cases the RECEIVER is "Pilate." The negative OBJECTS "non-response to accusation" and "non-justification of the accusation" (a stubborn repetition of the condemnation without explanation) are opposed to each other.

NP 9a vs. *NP 11a:* The RECEIVER (the "crowd") is the same. The OBJECTS are opposed to each other. In NP 9a the crowd receives a mandate from Pilate. The communication of this mandate is nothing other than a communication of volition; the crowd is called upon by Pilate to act according to *its own will*. This OBJECT is opposed to the one communicated in NP 11a; the chief priests in exciting the crowd call the latter to act according to the priests' will rather than according to the crowd's own will.

In the representation of this system of transformations we have organized the pertinent programs according to the logic of the narrative development. Since the narrative development is organized around the principal axis in verses 42 to 46, we have respected the order of the principal programs for this part of the text. Since in verses 1 to 37 the narrative development is organized around the polemical axis, we have respected the order of the polemical programs for this part of the text.

The Systems of Pertinent Transformations
of the Interpretative Narrative Levels

INTERPRETATIVE NARRATIVE LEVEL I (15:47—16:8)

The polemical axis is the shorter. Thus we first make a list of the polemical programs.

Narrative Manifestations	*Narrative Programs* (NP)
16:8b: They said nothing to anyone (also 7b, "go, tell his disciples and Peter . . .")	NP 16:7b, women (message about 8b: Jesus ⇸ Peter and disciples)
16:8a: They went out and fled from the tomb	NP 16:8a: women (far from the tomb → women)
16:6c: Do not be amazed	NP 16:6c: women (non-fear ⇸ women)
16:5c: They were amazed	NP 16:5c: women (fear → women)
16:3b: They were saying to one another, "Who will roll away the stone for us?"	NP 16:3b: women (information (?) about helper ⇸ women)

Remarks:

NP 16:7b, 8b: This program is already formulated in verse 7b, which manifests the contractual statement 1 (CS 1). NP 16:7b, 8b and NP 6c are clearly polemical because the text manifests their interruption (the non-transformation). If they had been realized they would have belonged to the principal axis. The text does not manifest as clearly the interruption of NP 16:3b. This is why we cannot be absolutely certain that it actually belongs to the polemical axis; it could eventually belong to the principal axis as the contractual statement of a suspended program in the following form: women (information about helper → women). We explored both possibilities without finding any program opposite to it.

Concerning the interpretation of the verbs expressing emotions and feelings (and also the interpretation of many reflexive verbs and certain verbs in the middle voice in Greek), let us note that emotion (in this case, fear) is at once an OBJECT which one communicates to oneself (thus the SUBJECT is responsible for his/her fear: one can say, "Do not fear") and a HELPER (i.e., something that the SUBJECT has received from someone or something else). This remark applies also to the cognitive verbs. When a SUBJECT says something to someone, this message is at once an OBJECT that he/she communicates and a HELPER that he/she has received (the SUBJECT needs to know what he/she is speaking about!).

In studying the principal axis of Interpretative Level I, we can then expose the following system of pertinent transformations:

NP 16:7e Jesus (message about Jesus → Peter and disciples)

*NP 16:7b, 8b women (message about Jesus ↛ Peter and disciples)

*NP 16:6b young man (mandate → women)

NP 16:5c women (fear → women)

*NP 16:5a women (inside of the tomb → women)

NP 16:8a women (far from the tomb ↛ women)

Remarks:

NP 16:7e vs. *NP 16:7b, 8b:* In both cases "the disciples and Peter" are the RECEIVERS, and the "message about Jesus in Galilee" is the OBJECT. In the first instance the performance is realized, in the second it is interrupted.

NP 16:6b vs. *NP 16:5c:* The "women" are the RECEIVERS in both programs. The OBJECTS are opposed to one another: in the one case the women receive the mandate asking them not to be afraid; in the other, they attribute fear to themselves.

NP 16:5a vs. *16:8a:* The "women" are the RECEIVERS in both programs. The OBJECTS "inside the tomb" and "far from the tomb" are opposed to one another.

We have organized these pertinent transformations according to the logic of the narrative development. The last program of the text (NP 16:7b, 8b) is polemical (since it is interrupted). Thus the polemical axis organizes the end of the narrative development. Yet the principal axis (and thus NP 16:6b and NP 16:5a) organizes the narrative development of what comes before.

INTERPRETATIVE NARRATIVE LEVEL II

This level includes interpretation of the crucified Jesus by the passersby, the chief priests and the scribes, the robbers, the centurion, and the women. The principal axis is a little shorter. Let us make a list of the principal programs.

Narrative Manifestations

41c: many other women who came up with him to Jerusalem

41b: ministered to him

41a: followed him (when in Galilee)

Narrative Programs (NP)

NP 41c: other women (other women → Jesus)

NP 41b: women (service → Jesus)

NP 41a: women (women → Jesus)

Narrative Manifestations	Narrative Programs (NP)
40: women looking on	NP 40: women (knowledge about Jesus' death → women)
39c: Truly this man was the Son of God	NP 39c: centurion (faith in Jesus as Son of God → centurion)
39b: he said	NP 39b: centurion (message about Jesus → X)
39a: The centurion saw that he thus breathed his last	NP 39a: centurion (knowledge about the way Jesus died → centurion)
31c: he cannot save himself	NP 31c: Jesus (nonsalvation → Jesus)
31b: he saved others	NP 31b: Jesus (salvation → others)
29b: you who would destroy the temple and build it in three days	NP 29b: Jesus (destruction and reconstruction → temple)

Remarks:

NP 41c is formulated in analogy to *NP 41a*. Another possible formulation would have been: other women, Jesus (Jerusalem → other women, Jesus).

NP 41a: Following (as disciple) is giving oneself to somebody.

NP 39c: Verse 39c in a subtle way manifests a transformation. Indeed, the adverb "truly" ($\dot{\alpha}\lambda\eta\theta\tilde{\omega}_S$) must be accounted for. It manifests that what follows expresses the centurion's conviction. In other words, the centurion (SUBJECT) makes his own (centurion as RECEIVER) the faith that Jesus is the Son of God (OBJECT).

NP 31c and NP 31b. These two programs belong to the principal axis because they are mocked by the chief priests and the scribes (who belong to the polemical axis).

NP 29b: The same reasoning also applies to this program.

Studying the polemical axis of Interpretative Level II, we can then establish the following system of pertinent transformations.

NP 41b women (service → Jesus)	{ NP 29a passersby (insults → Jesus) { NP 32e robbers (insults → Jesus)
NP 39c centurion (faith in Jesus → centurion)	NP 32d priests, scribes (faith in Jesus → priests, scribes)
{ NP 31b Jesus (salvation → others) { NP 31c Jesus (non-salvation → Jesus)	{ NP 30a Jesus (salvation → Jesus) { NP 30b Jesus (non-cross → Jesus) { NP 32b Jesus (non-cross → Jesus)

Remarks:

NP 41b vs. *NP 29a, NP 32e:* The RECEIVER ("Jesus") is the same. The OBJECTS are opposed to one another. In NP 41b the women give service to Jesus and in so doing honor him. By contrast, in NP 29a and in NP 32e the passersby and the robbers insult him. Thus, the "insults" are opposed to the "service."

NP 39c vs. *NP 32d:* The OBJECT ("faith in Jesus") is the same. The two RECEIVERS (the "centurion" and the "chief priests and scribes") are opposed in several ways; for example, the former belongs to the pagan world and the latter to the religious world.

NP 31b vs. *NP 30a:* The OBJECT ("salvation") is the same. The RECEIVERS, "others" and "Jesus," are different.

NP 31c vs. *NP 30b, NP 32b:* The RECEIVER ("Jesus") is the same. The OBJECTS, "non-salvation" and "deliverance from the cross," are opposed to one another.

NP 30a, NP 30b, and NP 32b, despite minor differences, are to be viewed as a "triplication" of the same program. Thus we shall consider this a single narrative opposition: NP 31b, NP 31c vs. NP 30a, NP 30b, NP 32b.

The order of the narrative development is clear in the case of the last two oppositions. The narrative development progresses on both axes from NP 31b, NP 31c vs. NP 30a, NP 30b, NP 32b toward NP 39c vs. NP 32d. We can consider that the narrative development is prolonged on the principal axis according to the order of the narrative manifestation. Indeed, NP 41b, which refers to the women following Jesus (as disciples) during his ministry in Galilee, applies also to the women after Jesus' death; Jesus' anointment, which they project, is a final "service" that they wish to render to him. Furthermore, serving Jesus implies a "faith in Jesus" comparable to the centurion's faith.[13] Thus the transformation of NP 41b can be viewed as prolonging the transformation of NP 39c. This is why we have organized the system of pertinent transformations as shown in the above figure.

INTERPRETATIVE NARRATIVE LEVEL III

This level concerns interpretation of Jesus' Aramaic message. The principal axis that is manifested by the enunciator's interpretation is shorter. In this sentence, four programs are manifested.

Narrative Manifestations	*Narrative Programs* (NP)
34e, d: hast thou forsaken me?	NP 34e: God (abandonment → Jesus)
	NP 34d: God (reason of abandonment → Jesus)

Narrative Manifestations	*Narrative Programs* (NP)
34c: my God, my God, why	NP 34c: Jesus (mandate → God)
34b: which means	NP 34b: enunciator (signification of Jesus' message → X)

Remarks:

NP 34c: As with any question, this one is a mandate given to someone, a mandate given by Jesus to God. The content of this program is a potential program: NP 34d. Furthermore, this question refers to a performance by God, abandoning Jesus (NP 34e).

In studying the polemical axis (manifested by vv. 35 and 36) we find the following system of pertinent transformations.

NP 34e: God (abandonment → Jesus)	NP 36g: Elijah (non-cross → Jesus)
NP 34c: Jesus (mandate → God)	NP 36d: a bystander (mandate → bystanders)

Remarks:

NP 34e vs. *NP 36g:* The RECEIVER ("Jesus") is the same. The OBJECTS, however, are opposed to one another: the "abandonment" of Jesus by God means death for Jesus; the "coming down from the cross" would mean life for him.

NP 34c vs. *NP 36d:* In both cases the OBJECT is a mandate establishing a program whose goal is to provide information about Jesus' situation. The RECEIVERS, God and the bystanders, are different.

An actual narrative development is found only on the polemical axis (the bystanders' story). Consequently, we organize this system of transformations according to this axis.

THE SYMBOLIC SYSTEM

The relations among the various systems of transformations of Mark 15:1—16:8 can now be represented as in Figure 9.

The system of transformations at the first interpretative level interprets and prolongs NP 46c (Joseph's action), the second prolongs NP 24a, 25 (the soldiers' action), and the third NP 34a (Jesus' cry).

In order to obtain the symbolic system, it is enough to slide upward the fourfold polemical axis. The programs NP 17a, NP 24a, 25, and NP 37a of the primary level participate both in the symbolic system of the primary

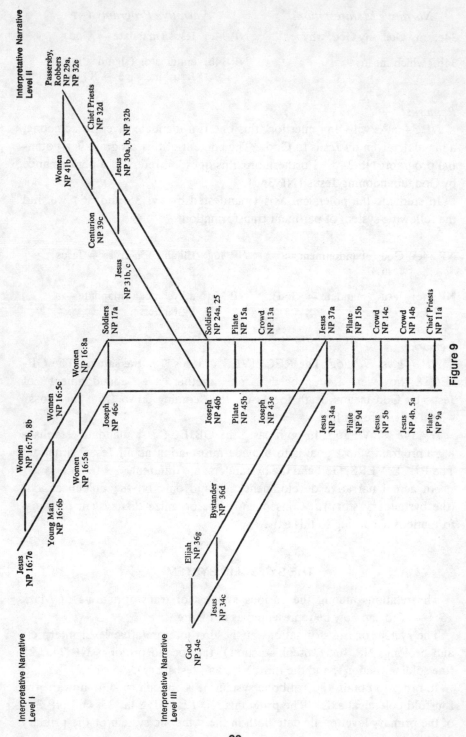

Interpretative Narrative Level I

Interpretative Narrative Level II

Interpretative Narrative Level III

Jesus
NP 16:7e

Young Man
NP 16:6b

Women
NP 16:7b, 8b

Women
NP 16:5c

Women
NP 16:8a

Women
NP 16:5a

Joseph
NP 46c

Soldiers
NP 17a

Jesus
NP 31b, c

Centurion
NP 39c

Women
NP 41b

Chief Priests
NP 32d

Jesus
NP 30a, b, NP 32b

Passersby, Robbers
NP 29a, NP 32e

Elijah
NP 36g

Bystander
NP 36d

Jesus
NP 34c

God
NP 34e

Soldiers
NP 24a, 25

Pilate
NP 15a

Crowd
NP 13a

Joseph
NP 46b

Pilate
NP 45b

Joseph
NP 43e

Jesus
NP 37a

Pilate
NP 15b

Crowd
NP 14c

Crowd
NP 14b

Chief Priests
NP 11a

Jesus
NP 34a

Pilate
NP 9d

Jesus
NP 5b

Jesus
NP 4h, 5a

Pilate
NP 9a

Figure 9

60

level and in one of the symbolic systems of the interpretative levels. They shift upward both in the primary narrative level and in the relevant interpretative level in order to be, in each case, in a contradictory relation with the program with which they are narratively opposed. We shall represent in separate diagrams the four parts of the symbolic system when it comes time to interpret them.

FROM THE SYMBOLIC SYSTEM TO THE SEMANTIC UNIVERSE

Together with its qualifications, the SUBJECT of each pertinent program is the symbolic expression of a semantic value (or state) that participates in the semantic universe presupposed by the text. Reading over the text, we now need to make a list of the qualifications of each SUBJECT. These qualifications are manifested as the investment of the actantial positions of HELPER (H), SENDER (S^{er}), and OPPONENT (OP) in a given program. The identification of these qualifications can be made without any problem.[14] For our present purposes it is sufficient to present in summary form the qualifications of each symbolic term in a first representation of each semiotic square.[15]

The following step of our exegesis aims at elucidating the symbolic value that each term symbolizes because of its intratextual relations. For this purpose we need to study the relations that this term has with the other terms of the semiotic squares to which it belongs. Of the many semantic features that each symbolic term possesses, only a few are pertinent. A study of the squares will allow us to identify them. The pertinent categories are established with rigor through the careful examination of the three types of relations in the semiotic square. Yet we do not express these categories with the same accuracy. The metalanguage used in order to designate these categories is necessarily an approximation. Other exegetes could eventually refer to the same symbolic values by means of a terminology other than ours. This is why we shall write, for instance, /silence vis-à-vis the accusations/, which should be read: symbolic value which can be expressed by the phrase "silence vis-à-vis the accusations."

Study of the Symbolic System of the Primary Level

The symbolic system of the primary level can be represented as in Figure 10.

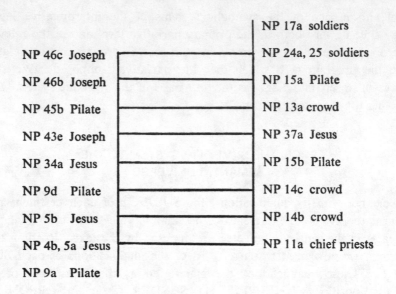

Figure 10

FIRST SQUARE

NP 5b *Jesus*	**NP 14b** *Crowd*
H: Pilate, silence	H: excitement produced by the chief
	priests, prisoner released at the
OP: (chief priests)	feast, shouts of condemnation
(chains)	Ser: Pilate
(accusations by chief priests)	OP: Pilate

NP 4b, 5a *Jesus*	**NP 11a** *Chief priests*
H: non-response to the accusations,	H: consultation, morning,
King of Jews	accusations, Pilate, envy
Ser: Pilate	
OP: chief priests, chains, accusations	OP: Jesus
of chief priests	

The pertinent semantic features of this first square are those designating certain attitudes related to the accusations. Jesus' silence (NP 5b) is in a contrary relation to the crowd's excitement (NP 14b). Jesus is silent vis-à-vis the chief priests' accusations, while the crowd is excited by the chief priests, who have uttered many accusations against Jesus. This /silence vis-à-vis the accusations/ is thus contrary to the /excitement related to the accusations/.

Jesus' silence (NP 5b) and the many accusations by the chief priests

(NP 11a) are contradictory. Jesus makes no further attempt to answer, even though Pilate reminds him of the many accusations brought against him. By contrast, the chief priests bring many accusations against Jesus (in order to excite the crowd). The /silence vis-à-vis the accusations/ is opposed to the /speech (non-silence) of accusations/.

The crowd's excitement in NP 14b is contradictory to Jesus' qualification in NP 4b, 5a. Even though he gives answer to Pilate, Jesus does not defend himself against the chief priests' accusations. This attitude manifests a /non-excitement vis-à-vis the accusations/ that is contradictory to the /excitement related to the accusations/ characterizing the crowd.

The subcontraries (NP 4b, 5a and NP 11a) oppose two types of speech: the /speech of accusations/ of the chief priests and the /speech without concern for the accusations/ of Jesus.

Thus we have a first square of symbolic values presupposed by the text (see Square 1).

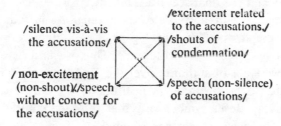

Square 1

The silence and the absence of concern for the accusations (even though one could defend oneself against these accusations) are therefore posited by the text as two attitudes with a positive value. By contrast, the excitement related to the accusations (the excitement provoked by the accusations and presupposing them) and the accusations (which are not established on the basis of a demonstration of their truth but on an emotional basis—such as envy—and which consequently demand an emotional response, such as excitement) are posited as having a negative value.

In anticipation of our discussion on the hermeneutics of Mark 15 and 16 (Chapter 4), let us note the hermeneutical implications of these initial conclusions. In our own experience we witness, or share in, many situations that involve these values. Is it so difficult to discover about us "emotional accusations" and the excitement related to such accusations? Our text designates them as negative values. Yet it also suggests that they are linked with the positive values of /silence/ and /absence of concern vis-à-vis the accusations brought against oneself/. Looking more closely at what happens about us, would it not be possible to discover the manifestation of these positive values in the attitude of some people?[16] Our culture that is characterized by competition would consider such persons to be fools who will never be successful. The text of Mark allows us to see these persons as the ones who manifest the gospel.

By studying the same square at another level, it is possible to show the relations among the symbols (or more precisely the thematic roles) "Jesus," "crowd," "Jesus as King of the Jews," and "chief priests" in order to define these symbols more precisely. For brevity's sake we shall present this study of the symbols only in a few instances where the symbols are particularly important.

Let us first of all consider the subcontraries. Jesus is qualified as /King of the Jews/. The chief priests represent a thematic role, which is posited by the text as opposed to /King of the Jews/. The chief priests (together with the scribes and the Pharisees) are members of the Sanhedrin, that is, they are associated with and represent a religious institution that has authority over the Jews. The kingship of Jesus is therefore directly opposed to this Jewish religious institution. Thus we find here the opposition between two types of authority over the Jewish people. Furthermore, the chief priests (as members of an institution) act only after consulting among themselves. Jesus symbolically manifests the contradictory value. He is alone. He is not a member of an institution. He is not priest. The opposition of the contraries can now be seen. It is the opposition /alone/ vs. /crowd/. Furthermore, /King of the Jews/ is defined as /non-crowd/; he is a personage different from the (common) people. (See Square 1 bis.)

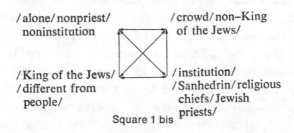

Square 1 bis

The relations of implication help us to define further the thematic roles. One characteristic of the "kingship of Jesus" is his solitude. By contrast, the "religious institution" is correlated with the crowd; without the crowd, without people over which it can exercise its power, the religious institution cannot exist. The kingship of Jesus appears most clearly when he is alone, abandoned by everybody. This becomes even clearer when we consider the symbolic values of this square. The solitude (of the King of the Jews) is associated with /silence/; the crowd (many people) with the /shouts of condemnation/; the kingship of Jesus with a quiet affirmation without concern for the accusations, while the religious institution affirms itself in a polemic (against Jesus) and in the manipulation of the crowd (exciting it).

SECOND SQUARE

NP 9d *Pilate*

H: astonishment, prisoner released at the feast, submission to the will of the crowd, volition to release the King of the Jews

S^er^: crowd

OP: chief priests

NP 14c *Crowd*

H: prisoner released at the feast, excitement produced by the chief priests, willingness that the King of the Jews be crucified, imposition of their will upon Pilate, refusal to give information, louder and louder shouts

OP: Pilate (hesitating)

NP 5b *Jesus*

H: Pilate, silence

OP: chief priests, chains, accusations by chief priests

NP 14b *Crowd*

H: excitement produced by the chief priests, prisoner released at the feast, shouts of condemnation

S^er^: Pilate

OP: Pilate

The second square manifests various attitudes related to the volition (or will) of the personages. Pilate's submission to the crowd's will (NP 9d) and the crowd's non-submission to Pilate's will (NP 14b) are contradictory. Pilate (NP 9d) would like to release the King of the Jews. Because he is amazed by Jesus' attitude, he asks the crowd what he should do. He does not himself make the decision but submits to the will of the crowd, all the while hoping that the crowd will be favorable to Jesus. By contrast, the crowd (NP 14b), which is excited by the chief priests, does not submit to Pilate's mandate. It does not answer his question. The /submission to the will of somebody/ is contradictory to the /non-submission to the will of somebody/.

The imposition of one's will as manifested by the crowd (NP 14c) and the nonimposition of one's will as manifested by Jesus (NP 5b) are contradictory. The crowd wants Pilate to obey a mandate that it gives to him. By contrast, Jesus does not answer Pilate. He does not try to convince Pilate; he does not impose his will upon him. The /imposition of one's will upon somebody/ is contradictory to the /non-imposition of one's will upon somebody/.

NP 9d and NP 14c are in contrary relation because Pilate submits to the crowd's will, and the crowd imposes its will upon Pilate.

The subcontraries have already been considered in our examination of the first square. Yet we need to examine them once again in order to define them further by considering their relations with the terms of the second square. Different semantic features may well be pertinent.

NP 5b and NP 14b are in contrary relation: Jesus by remaining silent does not impose his will; the crowd in not answering Pilate's question (a mandate) does not submit to his will. (See Square 2.)

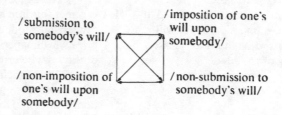

Square 2

We now recognize that the silence and the absence of concern vis-à-vis the accusations against oneself are posited as positive because the submission to somebody's will is also positive. The positive value /silence/ is not simply defined (cf. First Square) as the absence of concern for oneself (cf. the relation of implication), as the refusal to speak (cf. the contradictory) and as the refusal to condemn when excited (cf. the contrary), but also (cf. Second Square) as the refusal to impose one's will upon somebody (cf. the contradictory), that is, as the refusal to manipulate the will of others.[17] Similarly, the excitement related to the accusation and the accusations themselves are posited as negative values because they are aspects of the manipulation of the will of others (the imposition of one's will upon somebody) and also of the manipulation of the emotions of others (the excitement). We shall come back to the value /submission to somebody's will/ when dealing with the following squares.

The hermeneutical implications of our exegesis now become more exact. From the point of view of the Gospel narrative the various forms of /imposition of one's will upon somebody/ that we can witness in our society must be considered as the manifestations of negative values (whatever the value our society might give them), while the various forms of /submission to somebody's will/ must be considered as the manifestations of positive values. However, let us avoid any hasty generalization. These values will be defined more specifically through their relations with the values manifested in the other squares.

THIRD SQUARE

NP 34a *Jesus*

H: reaction against the crucifixion, message, cry, loud voice, ninth hour

OP: cross, chief priests, Pilate, crowd, robbers, passersby, soldiers

NP 15b *Pilate*

H: shouts of the crowd, willingness to give satisfaction to the crowd

S^{er}: crowd

OP: Jesus

NP 9d *Pilate*

H: astonishment, prisoner released at the feast, submission to the will of the crowd, volition to release the King of the Jews

S^{er}: crowd

OP: chief priests

NP 14c *Crowd*

H: prisoner released at the feast, excitement produced by the chief priests, willingness that the King of the Jews be crucified, imposition of their will upon Pilate, refusal to give information, louder and louder shouts

OP: Pilate (hesitating)

In the third square the pertinent investments concern power. NP 34a and NP 14c have in common the manifestation by a personage of his own will. Jesus (NP 34a) manifests his will (the will to know *why* God has abandoned him) and in a certain way attempts to impose it upon God (he wants an answer from God). The crowd (NP 14c) imposes its will upon Pilate. But contradictory values are associated with these two manifestations of the imposition of one's will. Jesus, who gives a mandate to God (NP 34a), is on the cross, annihilated by men. His message, uttered with a loud voice, is his last gasp; it actually shows Jesus to be /powerless/. This is contradictory to the value associated with the /imposition of one's will/ by the crowd upon Pilate (NP 14c) as a result of having been excited. This excitement is a form of power communicated to the crowd by the chief priests; this /power/ is manifested in the crowd's attitude toward Pilate. The /imposition of one's will though lacking power/ as symbolized by Jesus is contradictory to the /imposition of one's will, with power/ as symbolized by the crowd.

NP 15b and NP 9d both manifest Pilate as submitting to somebody's will. Nonetheless they are contradictory. On the one hand (NP 15b), Pilate submits because he /lacks will despite his power/ (he submits to the crowd which becomes more and more excited, yet he could exert his political power over this crowd, which resists his will). On the other hand (NP 9d), Pilate /submits to somebody's will/ because he is astonished by Jesus who does not defend himself against the chief priests' accusations; he is powerless as a result of Jesus' silence (how can he exert his power over somebody who does not resist!); he is /without power over Jesus/.

The /lack of will despite his power/ is contradictory to the /submission to somebody's will because one is powerless/ (over Jesus).

The /imposition of one's will although without power/ of Jesus (NP 34a) is contrary to the /lack of will despite his power/ of Pilate (NP 15b). Jesus reacts even though he is annihilated by the crucifixion, which has been imposed upon him by men. Pilate gives satisfaction to the crowd, thereby showing his lack of will before this ever-excited crowd even though he has power over the crowd because of his position.

NP 9d and NP 14c are contraries because Pilate, by submitting himself to the crowd, shows that he has no power over Jesus (NP 9d), while the excited crowd, by imposing its will upon Pilate, shows that it possesses (a type of) power (NP 14c). (See Square 3.)

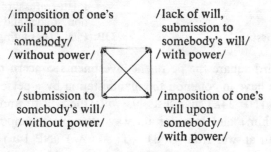

/ imposition of one's will upon somebody/ / without power/   /lack of will, submission to somebody's will/ /with power/

/ submission to somebody's will/ / without power/   /imposition of one's will upon somebody/ /with power/

Square 3

The submission to somebody's will is a positive value only insofar as it is associated with an absence of power, or more precisely, with a refusal to use the power that one has by becoming powerless (cf. Pilate's astonishment). It is not a submission because of a lack of will (which is a negative value). Indeed, in submitting himself to the crowd's will, Pilate has the will to release Jesus. The submission as positive value is correlated to the expression of one's own will (which confronts other people's will and eventually can be imposed upon them). Yet this affirmation of one's own will does not involve the use of power; it is associated with an absence of power. By contrast, the use of power (whatever the nature of this power might be) for the purpose of imposing one's will upon somebody—properly speaking manipulating somebody—is a negative value.

This square is a paradoxical[18] (non-logical) system of values that has the effect of strongly underlining the positive value of the *absence of power*, be it associated with a submission to somebody's will or with the imposition of one's will. Similarly, *having power* is posited as being negative, whether it is used (in order to impose one's will) or not used (by somebody who submits oneself to somebody else).

It is too early to draw the hermeneutical implications of this micro-system of values; these values will be further defined in the following squares. The role of a paradoxical square is to emphasize certain semantic features that are especially important (because they are surprising) and that are, in most instances, further defined in other squares.

FOURTH SQUARE

NP 43e *Joseph*
H: day of Preparation, day before the sabbath, respected member of the council, Pilate, courage, expectation of the kingdom of God

NP 37a *Jesus*
H: submission, loud cry, non-knowledge about why God abandoned him
OP: chief priests, Pilate, crowd, soldiers, robbers, cross with inscription, passersby, somebody, bystanders, abandoned by God

NP 34a *Jesus*
H: reaction against the crucifixion, message, cry, loud voice, ninth hour
OP: cross, chief priests, Pilate, crowd, robbers, passersby, soldiers

NP 15b *Pilate*
H: shouts of the crowd, will to give satisfaction to the crowd
S^{er}: crowd
OP: Jesus

In the fourth square the pertinent investments concern the relations between will (volition) and power. The isotopic space (i.e., what these two terms have in common) formed by NP 43e and NP 15b is organized around the semantic feature /power/. Joseph symbolizes religious /power/; he is a respected member of the council. Pilate symbolizes military or political /power/. The opposition religious vs. military (or political) is, however, not pertinent here (cf. the other relations of the square). The contradiction is established by the opposition /will/ vs. /lack of will/. Joseph is courageous and thus goes and asks Pilate for Jesus' body; he manifests his own /will/. Pilate submits to the crowd's will; he /lacks will/. The /will with power/ of Joseph is contradictory to the /lack of will with power/ of Pilate.

As noted above, in NP 34a Jesus manifests his own /will/ vis-à-vis God even though he is /powerless/. In NP 37a he is also /powerless/. But what does the inarticulate cry that precedes his expiration symbolize? The intratextual relations represented by the relations of the semiotic square demand that we understand this cry, and the expiration itself, as the *loss of his will*. Jesus who utters a loud cry (and expires) is not only /powerless/ but also /without will/. When this is recognized, one can then easily verify the other relations of the square and see that these values alone are pertinent (see Square 4).

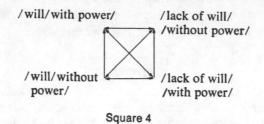

/will/with power/   /lack of will/
                                     /without power/

/will/without   /lack of will/
power/   /with power/

Square 4

This fourth square is also paradoxical.[19]   In this instance the semantic feature that is positively emphasized is the /will/. The lack of power is not in itself a positive value. It is the lack of power *associated with a volition* which is a positive value. In other words, it is a voluntary power-lessness, a refusal to make use of power. A lack of power coming from a lack of volition would be a negative value. Furthermore, the text posits the having of power as positive so long as it is associated with a volition, or better, so long as it is subordinated to a volition. The following square will show which specific type of volition has just such a positive value. Yet we can already say that the positive values /non-excitement/, /silence/, and /submission/ should in no way be interpreted as implying a lack of volition.

FIFTH SQUARE

NP 45b *Pilate*
H: knowledge about Jesus' death, centurion

S^{er}: Joseph

NP 13a *Crowd*
H: excitement produced by the chief priests, prisoner released at the feast, shouts

S^{er}: chief priests

NP 43e *Joseph*
H: day of Preparation, day before the sabbath, respected member of the council, Pilate, courage, expectation of the kingdom of God

NP 37a *Jesus*
H: submission, loud cry, non-knowledge about why God abandoned him

OP: chief priests, Pilate, crowd, soldiers, robbers, cross with inscription, passersby, bystanders, abandoned by God

In the fifth square the pertinent investments concern knowledge about death and deliverance. Pilate (NP 45b) has a /knowledge about the death of Jesus/. Once informed by the centurion of Jesus' death, he can give Joseph permission to take Jesus' body. This is contradictory to the /non-knowledge/ (the absence of knowledge) of Jesus about his own death (NP 37a). Jesus asks, "Why hast thou forsaken me?" because he does not know the "why" of his death and remains in ignorance. The /knowledge about Jesus' death/ symbolized by Pilate is contradictory to the /non-knowledge about Jesus' death/ symbolized by Jesus.

Joseph (NP 43e) and the crowd (NP 13a) have "expectation" in common. Joseph expects the kingdom of God; the crowd expects that Pilate will release a prisoner as he does at each (Passover) feast. In each case it is the expectation of a deliverance (given by God or by Pilate). Through considering the other relations of the square, it appears that the opposition "God vs. Pilate" is not pertinent here. These two types of expectation are also opposed according to the category of "knowledge." The hope for the kingdom of God that characterizes Joseph is a /non-knowledge/, since Joseph does not know when the kingdom of God will come, that is, when the deliverance will be given. This is contradictory to the /knowledge/ of the crowd about the deliverance of a prisoner; it takes place at each (Passover) feast. The /non-knowledge about deliverance/ (which will be brought about by the coming of the kingdom of God) is contradictory to the /knowledge about deliverance/ (which is expected of Pilate). Once this is seen, the verification of the other relations of the square does not present any difficulty (see Square 5).

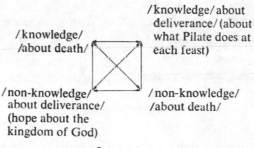

Square 5

This square defines the specific volition (or will) that previously has been marked as an important positive semantic feature. This volition is correlated with the hope concerning the kingdom of God. As would be anticipated in a narrative about the one who proclaims the coming of the kingdom of God (1:15), the volition that up until now undergirds all the values of the positive axis is a volition oriented and determined by the expectation of the kingdom of God. But the way in which this hope is defined is surprising. As is the case with the preceding values, the value given to this hope contradicts the expected systems of values. Is not the true believer someone who has a /knowledge about deliverance/? Is that not what faith is? No, answers our text. A knowledge about deliverance is actually a false knowledge (a knowledge that has a negative value) because it is a knowledge about a human deliverance (a deliverance promised and given by man).

This knowledge about deliverance implies (cf. the relation of implication) a /non-knowledge about death/ or, more specifically, a non-knowledge about the reason (the "why") of death. We could say that because of the knowledge about (human) deliverance, one cannot perceive the reality of death. Indeed, the knowledge about death (a concrete knowledge about the death of a person and not a general knowledge about death as a universal phenomenon) is a positive value. From the point of view of our text, the true believer accepts the fact of death. This knowledge about death implies a /non-knowledge about deliverance/; the expectation of the kingdom of God, a specific hope, is a /non-knowledge/ about true deliverance (the deliverance that comes from God).

There are many hermeneutical possibilities offered by the micro-system of values of this square. In anticipation of our hermeneutical remarks (Chapter 4), let us note that our society is characterized by a "non-knowledge about death" (death being rejected as outside of the "real world" because of its status as taboo) and a /knowledge about deliverance/ (e.g., medical techniques).[20] It is interesting to observe that our text invites us to oppose these values of our society not with a *knowledge* about a supernatural deliverance but with a knowledge about death correlated with a hope that is a non-knowledge about deliverance. The study of the sixth square will help us to be more specific.

Sixth Square

NP 46b *Joseph*	NP 15a *Pilate*
H: a respected member of the council, permission from Pilate, (money, storekeeper), linen shroud	H: lack of information about the wrongdoing that Jesus has committed
	OP: his own will
NP 45b *Pilate*	NP 13a *Crowd*
H: knowledge about Jesus' death, centurion	H: excitement given by the chief priests, prisoner released at the feast, shouts
Ser: Joseph	Ser: chief priests

In the sixth square the pertinent investments concern the relations between political and religious authorities. NP 46b and NP 13a have in common the semantic feature, /religious authority/. Joseph (NP 46b) is qualified as a "respected member of the council"; he symbolizes the religious authority. Furthermore, he asks and receives permission from Pilate and thus can take Jesus down from the cross in order to bury him. Therefore he recognizes the political authority of Pilate. This is contradictory to the symbol "crowd" (NP 13a), which acts with authority. Its authority is "religious" because it is given to the crowd by the chief priests (they are SENDERS). Furthermore, the crowd imposes its will upon Pilate. It asks no permission of Pilate! It does not recognize the political authority of Pilate. The /recognition of the political authority (of Pilate) by a religious authority/ (Joseph) is contradictory to the /non-recognition of the political authority (of Pilate) by a religious authority/ (the crowd as depository of the chief priests' authority).

NP 45b and NP 15a have in common /non-submission to the religious authority/. Pilate (NP 45b) gives an order to the centurion so that he might obtain information about the death of Jesus. Thus he manifests his authority over the centurion. Furthermore, by mandating the centurion, Pilate shows that he does not submit to the religious authority of Joseph, who comes and asks for Jesus' body. This is contradictory to Pilate in NP 15a, who does not use his political authority (which gives him the right to give orders to the crowd). But the fact that he asks what wrongdoing Jesus has committed shows that Pilate does not (yet) submit to the religious authority of the crowd (as depository of the chief priests' authority). The /exerted political authority, not submitted to the religious authority/ symbolized by Pilate (NP 45b), is contradictory to the /non-exerted political authority, not submitted to the religious authority/ symbolized by Pilate (NP 15a).

The values presupposed by these four terms may be represented, in a first approximation, as in Square 6a.

Before considering the relations of contrariety, let us first note that in this square different types of authority are marked either positively as recognized, exerted, and accepted, or negatively as not recognized, not exerted, and not accepted.

NP 45b and NP 13a are contraries because Pilate symbolizes (NP 45b) the political authority marked positively (exerted) and the religious authority negatively (not recognized), while the crowd symbolizes (NP 13a) the political authority marked negatively (not recognized) and the religious authority positively (accepted).

NP 46b and NP 15a are contraries because Joseph symbolizes (NP 46b) the political authority (which is recognized) and the religious authority

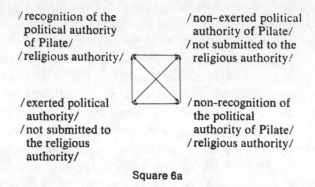

/recognition of the
  political authority
  of Pilate/
/religious authority/

/non-exerted political
  authority of Pilate/
/not submitted to the
  religious authority/

/exerted political
  authority/
/not submitted to
  the religious
  authority/

/non-recognition of
  the political
  authority of Pilate/
/religious authority/

Square 6a

(qualification of Joseph), both marked positively, while Pilate symbolizes (NP 15a) the political authority (which is not exerted) and the religious authority (which is not recognized), both marked negatively.

These observations allow us to represent the square as in Square 6b,

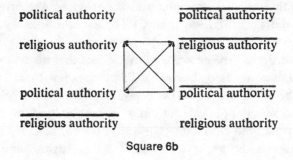

political authority

~~political authority~~

religious authority

~~religious authority~~

political authority

~~political authority~~

~~religious authority~~

religious authority

Square 6b

which shows that it is paradoxical. It has the effect of strongly emphasizing the semantic feature "political authority" as being positive (whether it is positively associated with the religious authority or not). The formulation of this feature is only approximate. The term "political" attempts to account for the fact that this authority is related to the secular organization (in contrast to the religious organization) of the society. The positive value /knowledge about death/ is therefore correlated with a political authority that does not recognize the religious authority. In other words, the knowledge about death (a decisive value since it is presupposed by the hope about the kingdom of God) belongs to the secular order. Thus, according to our text, the hope about the kingdom of God is necessarily rooted in a secular knowledge.

Beyond the positive value that this square attributes to the secular, it posits the political authority (which maintains the secular order) as a positive value, whether or not it is in good relation with the religious authority. Furthermore, political authority has a negative value as soon as it does not assume its role, either because of reasons unconnected with religious authority or because of its submission to religious authority. One final remark about this square: The religious authority assumes its proper place when it recognizes political authority (although this does not necessarily imply a submission) and it does not assume its proper place when exerting its power over political authority (i.e., when substituting itself for the political authority by not recognizing it).

SEVENTH SQUARE

NP 46c *Joseph*	NP 24a, 25 *Soldiers*
H: linen shroud, Jesus (down from the cross)	H: Jesus (received from Pilate), crown of thorns, acclamations, blows with a reed, spittle, kneeling position, mocking, cross with inscription, Simon of Cyrene, Golgotha, wine mingled with myrrh, third hour
	OP: Jesus
NP 46b *Joseph*	NP 15a *Pilate*
H: respected member of the council, permission from Pilate, (money, storekeeper), linen shroud	H: lack of information about what wrongdoing Jesus has committed
	OP: his own will

In the seventh square the pertinent investments concern various attitudes toward authority. Joseph (NP 46c) has asked and received permission to take Jesus' body in order to bury him. His attitude demonstrates his /respect for Jesus/. By contrast, the soldiers (NP 24a, 25) who crucify Jesus according to Pilate's order have a contemptuous attitude toward Jesus; they insult him, mock him, and salute him as King of the Jews, while striking him and spitting on him. /Respect for Jesus/ (NP 46c) is contrary to /contempt for the King of the Jews/ (NP 24a, 25).

The soldiers (NP 24a, 25) are contradictory to Joseph (NP 46b). By asking Pilate's permission Joseph manifests his recognition of Pilate's political authority. We may therefore say that Joseph's attitude is an attitude of /non-contempt for Pilate/. This is another way of expressing the value /recognition of the political authority/ of Pilate (cf. the preceding square), which is a positive attitude toward Pilate yet not a "respectful" attitude (in the strong sense that this phrase has when describing Joseph's attitude toward Jesus). The contradiction "soldiers vs. Joseph" is therefore manifested by the opposition /contempt/ vs. /noncontempt/. In this contradiction, the phrases "King of the Jews" and "political authority" (of Pilate) can be used to define the isotopic space (i.e., what these two terms have in common). Thus, in this instance the phrase "King of the Jews" symbolizes the political authority of Jesus. The contradiction can be formulated as follows: /contempt for the political authority (of Jesus)/ (NP 24a, 25) vs. /recognition of the political authority (of Pilate)/ (NP 46b).

The opposition of contrariety, NP 46b vs. NP 15a, which has been considered in the preceding square, can be formulated anew as the opposition /non-contempt (recognition) for political authority/ vs. /non-respect (non-recognition) for religious authority/.

Pilate (NP 15a) symbolizes the /non-respect (non-submission) for religious authority/. This is contradictory to the /respect for Jesus/ on Joseph's part (NP 46c). The contradiction is manifested by the opposition /respect/ vs. /non-respect/. Thus in this contradiction, "Jesus" and the "religious authority" define the isotopic space. Here "Jesus" is considered a religious authority.[21] The contradiction is: /respect for the religious authority/ (of Jesus) vs. /non-respect for the religious authority/ (of Jesus).

The values presupposed by these four terms may be represented, in a first approximation, by Square 7a.

respect for Jesus
(for Jesus' religious
authority)

contempt for the
King of the Jews
(for Jesus' political
authority)

non-contempt for
Pilate (for Pilate's
political authority)

non-respect
(non-submission) for
the religious
authority (of the
crowd as depository
of the chief priests'
authority)

Square 7a

The pertinent semantic features (i.e., the features that set the terms in the threefold relations of the semiotic square) are quite broad. The square manifests the relations among various attitudes toward the religious and political authorities. Neither the difference between Jesus' religious authority and the chief priests' religious authority nor the difference between Pilate's political authority and Jesus' political authority (as King of the

Jews) is pertinent here. The pertinent values may then be represented as in Square 7b, which clearly shows that we are dealing with a paradoxical

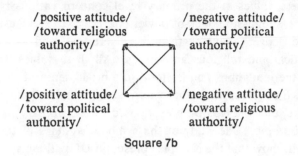

/positive attitude/ /toward religious authority/ — /negative attitude/ /toward political authority/

/positive attitude/ /toward political authority/ — /negative attitude/ /toward religious authority/

Square 7b

square.[22] As such, this square emphasizes that the positive attitudes toward the authority are positive values, whether this authority be political or ·religious. The square also emphasizes that the negative attitudes toward the authority (whether political or religious) are negative values. Let us also note that the recognition of political authority is subordinated to that of religious authority. Thus the recognition of political authority by religious authority (a positive value identified in the preceding square) does not presuppose an unconditional submission to political authority. The recognition of political authority is a positive value only insofar as it also implies a respect for religious authority. This type of respect is manifested in the text both by Joseph's actions and by Joseph's acceptance of Jesus' teaching about the coming of the kingdom of God.

On the negative axis, let us note that the non-submission to religious authority implies the non respect for political authority. In other words, the non-respect for political authority is one of the various manifestations of non-submission to religious authority. This observation underscores the importance, for the believer, of a positive attitude toward political authority.

It is noteworthy that the kind of political authority (i.e., whether it is legitimate or not) and the quality of the religious authority (i.e., whether it is authentic or not) are not taken into consideration in this square. Is this to say that the types of political or religious authority are irrelevant and that the Gospel presupposes that a positive attitude toward these authorities always has a positive value? Such a conclusion would hardly fit the rest of the Gospel, which describes conflicts between Jesus and the established Jewish authorities. We must therefore conclude that the values of this square presuppose more fundamental values, which define true religious authority and its relationship to political authority. Thus we shall not be surprised to find these more fundamental values manifested at the interpretative levels. This remark also applies to each of the squares at the primary level. They define a series of values that are secondary; they need to be further defined through their relations with more fundamental values. These values at the primary level concern various types of attitudes: silence, submission, lack of power (or refusal to make use of power), volition, knowledge (about death and deliverance), and various attitudes toward political and religious authorities. All these values belong to the category of the modalities (understood in a broad sense of the term), i.e., of the values that presuppose other values and "modulate" them.[23] We can say, therefore, that the isotopy presupposed by the primary narrative level is a *modal isotopy*. The study of the symbolic systems of the interpretative levels will show that the isotopies presupposed by these systems involve a series of values which are more fundamental. They establish, among other things, what is authentic religious authority.

Study of the Symbolic System of Interpretative Level III

The symbolic system[24] of Interpretative Level III can be represented as in Figure 11.

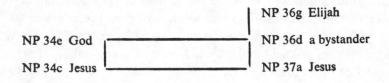

NP 34e God

NP 34c Jesus

NP 36g Elijah

NP 36d a bystander

NP 37a Jesus

Figure 11

There is only one square, which we now represent in its symbolic form.

NP 34e *God*

NP 36d *A bystander*
H: quickness, Jesus' Aramaic message, reed, sponge full of vinegar

NP 34c *Jesus*
H: cry, loud voice, ninth hour, Aramaic message addressed to God
OP: chief priests, robbers, passersby, soldiers, Pilate, crowd, cross with inscription, knowledge about the abandonment by God

NP 37a *Jesus*
H: submission, loud cry, non-knowledge about why God abandoned him
OP: chief priests, Pilate, crowd, soldiers, robbers, cross with inscription, passersby, bystanders, abandonment by God

In this square the pertinent investments concern the relationship with

God. NP 34e and NP 37a are contradictory. Jesus (NP 37a) is not in relation with God; when he expires, the abandonment by God is fully manifested (up to that time he simply has a knowledge about his abandonment by God, which could be a true or a false knowledge). He is, therefore, /without God/. His mortality is also manifested; this symbolizes that he is /non-God/ (the contradictory of /God/).

NP 34c and NP 36d have Jesus' message in Aramaic in common. Jesus (NP 34c) invokes God's presence by means of a prayer (Ps. 22:2, in Aramaic). Thus he sets himself /in relation with God/. This is contradictory to the symbol "bystander" (NP 36d), who misinterprets what Jesus says. He does not understand that Jesus is addressing God. Being unable to recognize the call to God, the bystander manifests an absence of relation with God: he is a /man not in relation with God/. When this is recognized, the various relations of the semiotic square appear clearly (see Square, Level III).

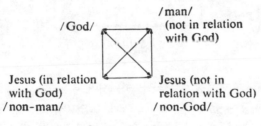

Square, Level III

The square of Interpretative Level III manifests the fundamental opposition "God vs. man." As would be expected, this opposition has "Jesus crucified" as its semantic mediation, however, not the negative symbol "Jesus crucified not in relation with God" but the positive symbol "Jesus crucified in relation with God." Indeed, his opponents view "Jesus dying on the cross" as the manifestation of a lack of relationship with God. Affirming this value for Jesus' death on the cross would resolve the fundamental opposition God vs. man in favor of man! It would mean "pleasing men" as Paul says in Galatians 1:10. The true mediation is "Jesus crucified," who manifests a relation with God. Even though he is annihilated by men, and powerless, even though he knows that he is abandoned by God, he remains in relation with God through his prayer. This is why he is the mediation between God and man (who is separated from God). This is why he is "non-man." Remaining in relation with God while knowing (or believing) that one is abandoned by God is a most unusual attitude for a man. It is being "Son of God," as the centurion confesses in our text (cf. the following squares).

Study of the Symbolic System of Interpretative Level II

This symbolic system can be represented as in Figure 12.

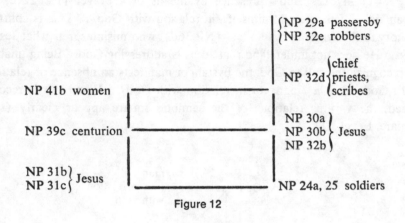

Figure 12

FIRST SQUARE

NP 39c *Centurion*	**NP 30a, NP 30b, NP 32b *Jesus***
H: knowledge about the way Jesus died, faith in Jesus as Son of God, before Jesus	H: destruction and reconstruction of the temple, mandate of the passersby (salvation for himself), Christ, King of Israel
	S^er: passersby, chief priests, scribes
NP 31b, NP 31c *Jesus*	**NP 24a, 25 *Soldiers***
H: salvation for others, non-salvation for himself, King of the Jews	H: Jesus (received from Pilate), crown of thorns, acclamations, blows with a reed, spittle, kneeling position, mocking, cross with inscription, Simon of Cyrene, Golgotha, wine mingled with myrrh, third hour
OP: chief priests, passersby, robbers, soldiers, insults, cross	OP: Jesus

In this square the pertinent investments concern the attitudes toward others and the relations between the Romans and the Jews. In NP 31b, NP 31c, on the one hand, and in NP 30a, NP 30b, NP 32b, on the other hand, Jesus is qualified by the same title: "King of the Jews" (cf. the inscription on the cross and the declaration of the chief priests and the scribes, "Christ, King of Israel").[25] In studying the various relations of the square we discover that, here, the only pertinent semantic feature is /Jew/. It is opposed to the semantic feature /Roman/ around which the isotopic space formed by NP 39c and NP 24a, 25 is organized. These semantic features will become more specific in the following square. The contradictory oppositions are established in the two isotopic spaces by the opposition /altruistic/ vs. /selfish/, or better yet, /other-centered/ vs. /self-centered/. Jesus (NP 31b, NP 31c), qualified as having saved others, is /other-centered/. Similarly, the centurion (NP 39c), qualified as being attentive to the way in which Jesus died, cares for what is happening to Jesus; thus he manifests the semantic feature /other-centered/. By contrast, the hypothetical Jesus (NP 30a, NP 30b, NP 32b) should save himself, should care for himself, that is, he should be /self-centered/. Similarly, the soldiers (NP 24a, 25) are before all else preoccupied with what they will be able to obtain for themselves (as is emphasized in the text by the description—between two references to the crucifixion process —of the way in which they divide his garments among themselves by casting lots). Thus we can say that they are /self-centered/. In the representation in Square 1, Level II the other relations of the square appear clearly.

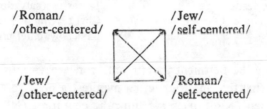

/Roman/   /Jew/
/other-centered/   /self-centered/

/Jew/   /Roman/
/other-centered/   /self-centered/

Square 1, Level II

This paradoxical square shows that the Roman as well as the Jew belongs to the positive axis of the system—which could be termed "mythical system gospel" or better, using Jesus' terminology, "mythical system kingdom"—insofar as he is /other-centered/ (i.e., insofar as he cares for others) and also not self-centered (without preoccupation for his own fate). The ideal Jew—that is, Jesus as King of the Jews—is the one who saves others but does not do anything to save himself. By contrast, the Jew (even if he is the King of Israel) belongs to the negative axis as well as the Roman when he adopts a selfish attitude that necessarily involves his not truly caring for others. Indeed, the square posits the incompatibility of a self-centered attitude with a truly "caring for others" attitude. Either one lives "for oneself" and therefore one does not really live "for others," or one lives "for others" and therefore one totally renounces oneself.

The Passion according to Mark presupposes that there is no possible compromise between "being for others" and "being for oneself." If a compromise had been possible, there would not have been a Passion. Jesus would have used for himself the power that he had manifested when saving others. These values presupposed by the Passion have been emphasized and proclaimed on many occasions without ceasing to be felt as deeply paradoxical, and to be betrayed in favor of various types of compromises.

SECOND SQUARE

NP 41b *Women*

H: knowledge about Jesus' death, from afar, Jesus (in Galilee), service

NP 32d *Chief priests, scribes*

H: Jesus, Christ, King of Israel, coming down from the cross, faith in this Christ

OP: Jesus giving salvation to others and non-salvation to himself

NP 39c *Centurion*

H: knowledge about the way Jesus died, faith in Jesus as Son of God, before Jesus

NP 30a, NP 30b, NP 32b *Jesus*

H: destruction and reconstruction of the temple, mandate of the passersby (salvation for himself), Christ, King of Israel

S^{er}: passersby, chief priests, scribes

In this square the pertinent investments concern various classes of the society. Note first that the four terms manifest a positive attitude toward Jesus: the women (NP 41b) serve him; the centurion (NP 39c) believes in him; the chief priests and the scribes (NP 32b) (as SUBJECTS of the hypothetical program which presupposes that Jesus has come down from the cross) have faith in him; the hypothetical Jesus (NP 30a, NP 30b, NP 32b) saves himself. The system of values manifested by this square belongs as a whole to the semantic field of the positive attitudes toward Jesus.

NP 41b and NP 30a, NP 30b, and NP 32b have the semantic feature /Israel/ in common. The women represent the Jewish society (of Galilee), that is, the /common of the people of Israel/. This is contradictory to what is represented by Jesus (according to the chief priests, the scribes, and the passersby); as "Christ, King of Israel" he is the /chief of the people of Israel/. The contradiction opposes, therefore, two types of members of the people of Israel. Let us note that the isotopic space (i.e., what is common to both terms of a contradiction) is defined by two semantic features: /people/, which will be defined by the other relations of the square as /secular/ (i.e., as not belonging to the religious institution), and /Israel/ or /Jew/.

NP 32d and NP 39c have in common the semantic feature /chief/. The chief priests and the scribes are /chiefs of the Jewish religious institution/, while the centurion is /chief of a Roman secular institution/ (a section of the Roman army). The contradiction is established by the opposition /Jewish religious institution/ vs. /Roman secular institution/. Two semantic features are opposed: /religious/ vs. /secular/ (non-religious); /Jew/ vs. /Roman/. For the first time (we shall find other cases of this) we have a square that involves three pertinent semantic features for each term. (See Square 2, Level II.)

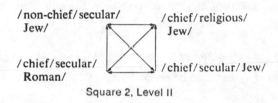

Square 2, Level II

The contraries "women" and "chief priests and scribes" are opposed to one another in two sets of semantic features: /non-chief/ vs. /chief/ and /secular/ vs. /religious/. The subcontraries "centurion" and "Jesus" are opposed to one another in the semantic features /Roman/ vs. /Jew/.

This square establishes the value that is to be assigned to various classes of the society in their positive relation to Jesus. The social classes that are in relation with Jesus according to the norms set by the system of values "gospel" have a positive value. These are the classes that, from the traditional Jewish point of view, were at the bottom of the social hierarchy:

(a) Those who, among the Chosen People, are the most secular, the furthest removed from the religious institution (symbolized by Jerusalem); and since they are Galileans, those who are the most deprived of political power (they are not only common people but also women!). These common people are now at the top of the new social hierarchy.

(b) Those who do not belong to the Chosen People, who oppose the Jewish political power, and who, of course, are not religious; in short, despised and hated enemies. They are now clearly set on the positive side of the new social hierarchy.[26]

By contrast, those who, from the traditional Jewish point of view, were at the top of the social hierarchy are now posited as having a negative value:

(a) The chief priests and the scribes (the religious leaders) wait for a false messiah. We might say that they manifest an antigospel (with reference to our study of Gal. 1:1–10 in Chapter 4 of *What Is Structural Exegesis?*).

(b) The Jewish political (i.e., secular) leaders cannot but become false messiahs (such as the hypothetical Jesus that the chief priests and the scribes envision) who first act for themselves and then eventually for others.

The hermeneutical possibilities opened up by these conclusions are readily perceived; it is enough to substitute the name of the new Chosen People for the term "Jew" and the name of the political power (or movement), which does not belong to the new Chosen People, for the term "Roman."

Study of the Symbolic System of Interpretative Level I

This symbolic system can be represented as in Figure 13.

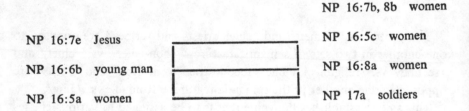

Figure 13

FIRST SQUARE

NP 16:6b *Young Man*

H: inside the tomb, sitting on the right side, dressed in a white robe, presence of the women, knowledge about the women's fear, knowledge that Jesus is risen, knowledge that Jesus is in Galilee

NP 16:8a *Women*

H: knowledge that Jesus is not here, empty place, tomb, knowledge about the presence of the young man, knowledge about the young man's message (Jesus is risen), trembling, astonishment

OP: fear

NP 16:5a *Women*

H: knowledge about where Jesus is, knowledge about the rolled stone, tomb, spices, after the sabbath, early morning, first day of the week

NP 17a *Soldiers*

H: Jesus (to be crucified), inside the palace, the whole battalion, purple cloak

S^{er}: Pilate

In this square the pertinent investments have to do with various attitudes toward the relation between two "spaces": the relations between the "world" of the living, /society/, and a "beyond the world of the living," an /outside of society/. NP 16:6b and NP 17a have the semantic feature /inside/ in common. The young man (NP 16:6b) is inside the tomb, that is, at the center of the "outside of society." He belongs to this realm outside of society, and thus he is in his own realm. He is also in the presence of the women (who here symbolize society). Furthermore, he announces that Jesus who was dead (and as such belongs to the realm "outside of society" and not to the world of the living) is going to Galilee, thus to a space in society. It follows that both through what he symbolizes and through what he announces, the young man is the manifestation of a positive attitude toward the relation "outside of society/society." Note that this relation is oriented from "outside of society" toward "society" (according to the point of view of the young man and also according to the orientation of Jesus' movement from one space to the other). Thus NP 16:6b manifests the semantic features: /outside of society/, /in his own realm/, /relation between the two spaces/, /orientation from outside of society to society/. This is contradictory to what is symbolized by the soldiers (NP 17a). They are inside the palace, that is, in a place representing the center of secular society, fully separated from the tomb. They manifest the following semantic features: /society/, /in their own realm/, /no relation between the two spaces/. We could add /orientation from society to outside of society/; this would be the orientation of the relation (if it were to take place) from the point of view of the soldiers, since they are in society. The isotopic space is organized around the semantic feature /in one's own realm/. The contradiction is manifested by the twofold opposition of the semantic features /outside of society/relation between the two spaces/ vs. /society/non-relation between the two spaces/.

NP 16:5a and NP 16:8a have the semantic feature /Jewish society/ in common. In both cases the women symbolize /Jewish society/ (because it is specified that they have waited for the end of the sabbath before buying the spices in order to anoint Jesus), which must be understood here as /religious (Jewish) society/. The women (NP 16:5a) know that the stone is rolled away and enter voluntarily into the tomb in order to anoint Jesus. Thus they have access to the tomb and manifest the volition of a conjunction of "society" with "outside of society." Thus NP 16:5a manifests the following semantic features: /society/, /religious/, /relation between the two spaces/, /orientation from society to outside of society/. The women (NP 16:8a), as members of the Jewish religious society, learn from the young man that Jesus (who, from the point of view of the women, belongs to outside of society, that is, the tomb) is no longer in the tomb, that he is risen, that he is going to Galilee (in society) despite the fact that, according to their expectation, he should be in the tomb. Their trembling and great fear symbolize a refusal to recognize the relation of "outside of society" with "society." While they (NP 16:5a) have accepted (indeed, have wanted) a relation of society with outside of society, they do not accept this relation with the opposite orientation. For the women it is normal to go and anoint a dead person. But the one who belongs to the realm of the dead should stay there and should not go into society. The women (NP 16:8a) manifest the following semantic features: /society/, /religious/, /refusal of the relation between the two spaces/, /orientation from outside of society to society/. The isotopic space formed by NP 16:5a and NP 16:8a is organized around the semantic features /society/ and /religious/. The contradiction is manifested by the twofold opposition of the semantic features /relation between the two spaces/ orientation from society to outside of society/ vs. /non-relation between the two spaces/orientation from outside of society to society/.

NP 16:5a and NP 17a are contraries because the women want a relation between society and outside of society while the soldiers, who are inside the palace, manifest the absence of relation between these two spaces.

NP 16:6b and NP 16:8a are contraries because the young man (NP 16:6b) represents the acceptance of the relation between outside of society and society, while the women refuse to accept this relation.

Despite the complexity of this square (each of its terms involving four pertinent features), it can be seen that it is a paradoxical square. It emphasizes that the relation between society and outside of society (whatever may be its orientation) is a positive value, while the absence of this relation or the refusal to accept it is a negative value. Let us note also that the opposition "life vs. death" (which we would have expected to find in the story of the Resurrection) is pertinent neither in this square nor in the following one. Our study of the relations of the square also shows that the tomb symbolizes not the "world of the dead"

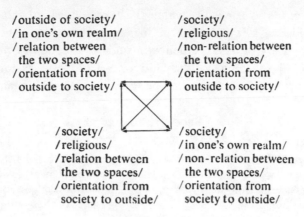

/outside of society/
/in one's own realm/
/relation between
the two spaces/
/orientation from
outside to society/

/society/
/religious/
/non-relation between
the two spaces/
/orientation from
outside to society/

/society/
/religious/
/relation between
the two spaces/
/orientation from
society to outside/

/society/
/in one's own realm/
/non-relation between
the two spaces/
/orientation from
society to outside/

Square 1, Level I

but more generally what is beyond human society (or even what is beyond the human realm); we can term this the "transcendent." Once this is recognized, the values interrelated in this square stand out more clearly.

Society represented by the soldiers is posited as having a negative value because it is not in relation with the transcendent; it ignores it. As such it is a *secular* society (in a pejorative sense).

Jewish society, or more generally the "religious" society, is defined as a society for which a relation of society with "outside of society" (with this orientation) is normal. Jewish society can and does approach the transcendent. As such, religious society has a positive value. By contrast, Jewish (or religious) society has a negative value when it refuses to accept this relation with its reversed orientation. When the transcendent approaches the human world of its own initiative, it brings on fear. This fear manifests a negative attitude toward the irruption of the transcendent in society. Indeed such an irruption should bring on a positive amazement, a marveling and a glorification of God, as the Gospel of Mark expresses on several occasions (for instance, in Mark 1:12 and 5:20; note also that the young man says to the women, "Do not be afraid"). According to our text, Jewish religion—but is this not true of other religions?—tragically limits the religious attitude to the believer's approach to the transcendent and consequently is unable to recognize the manifestations of the transcendent in society. By contrast, the system of values of our text underscores the fact that a religious attitude implies that the transcendent takes the initiative to establish a relation between itself and human society by intervening within it (otherwise, we might say, the religious attitude would be vain).

Our text posits as a positive value the transcendent in relation to the human world and as intervening in society. This value that is presupposed by the story of Jesus' crucifixion and resurrection is merely a reexpression of the theology of the God who acts in the history of Israel (and so in human history) that is to be found in the Old Testament.

SECOND SQUARE

NP 16:7e *Jesus*

H: of Nazareth, crucifixion, knowledge about the resurrection, message given to the disciples in Galilee

NP 16:5c *Women*

H: knowledge that the stone has been rolled away, inside the tomb, knowledge about the presence of the young man, fear

NP 16:6b *Young Man*

H: inside the tomb, sitting on the right side, dressed in a white robe, presence of the women, knowledge about the women's fear, knowledge that Jesus is risen, knowledge that Jesus is in Galilee

NP 16:8a *Women*

H: knowledge that Jesus is not here, empty place, tomb, knowledge about the presence of the young man, knowledge about the young man's message (Jesus is risen), trembling, astonishment

OP: fear

In this square the pertinent investments have to do with the relations between the knowledge about the resurrection and the categories of the preceding square. NP 16:7e and NP 16:8a have a /knowledge about Jesus' resurrection/ in common. Jesus' (NP 16:7e) announcing his resurrection to the disciples is qualified by a knowledge about what it is he announces. The fact that he is qualified as being from Nazareth underscores his /humanness/. It is the man Jesus who predicts his resurrection for the disciples. When he speaks to them, as well as when the young man speaks to the women, he is /in society/ (either with his disciples or in Galilee). This is contradictory to the women (NP 16:8a) who symbolize the /human/ in the tomb, in the /outside of society/. They have been told by the young man that Jesus is not in the tomb, that he is risen. They have, therefore, a /knowledge about Jesus' resurrection/. The /human in society with a knowledge about Jesus' resurrection/ is therefore contradictory to the /human outside of society with a knowledge about Jesus' resurrection/. The latter situation is qualified as being negative; human beings with a knowledge of Jesus' resurrection when outside their own realm are struck with fear and trembling. This is not the case for human beings with a knowledge about Jesus' resurrection when within their own realm.

NP 16:6b and NP 16:5c have the semantic feature "inside the tomb" or /outside of society/ in common. The young man (NP 16:6b) dressed in a white robe is sitting on the right side in the tomb. He symbolizes the /non-human/. Furthermore, he knows that Jesus is risen (content of his speech). This is contradictory to what is symbolized by the women (NP 16:5c) in the tomb (human in the outside of society), who do not (yet) know that Jesus is risen. The /non-human outside of society with a knowledge about Jesus' resurrection/ is contradictory to the /human outside of society without knowledge about Jesus' resurrection/. The latter situation is qualified as being negative; the women are afraid.

NP 16:7e and NP 16:5c are in a relation of contrariety because Jesus represents the /human in society with a knowledge about the resurrection/, while the women represent the /human outside of society without knowledge about the resurrection/.

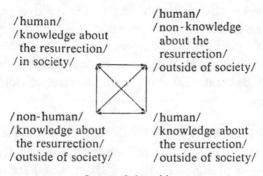

/human/
/knowledge about
the resurrection/
/in society/

/human/
/non-knowledge
about the
resurrection/
/outside of society/

/non-human/
/knowledge about
the resurrection/
/outside of society/

/human/
/knowledge about
the resurrection/
/outside of society/

Square 2, Level I

Thus the fact of having a knowledge about the resurrection is positive only when one is in one's own milieu. The fact of not being in one's own milieu is negative whether or not one has a knowledge about the resurrection. Thus a knowledge about Jesus' resurrection is accepted by the "human" in society and by the "non-human" in the outside of society. A knowledge about Jesus' resurrection is a true knowledge only for those who are in their own milieu.

By contrast, for human beings outside of society (not in their own milieu) the only possibility is fear, whether or not they have a knowledge about Jesus' resurrection.

We can conclude from this that there are two legitimate types of knowledge about Jesus' resurrection:

(1) The knowledge that the transcendent (the young man and eventually God) has; this knowledge about Jesus' resurrection can be acquired in the "outside of society" when it is one's own milieu. A "transcen-

dent" knowledge about the resurrection (from God's perspective) is thus considered to be legitimate.

(2) The knowledge that human beings can have; this knowledge about Jesus' resurrection is acquired by them in their own milieu, that is, in socicty.

By contrast, a knowledge about Jesus' resurrection by human beings in the "outside of society" is necessarily a false knowledge; it engenders fear. For instance, it is misleading to believe that human beings can acquire "true" knowledge about the resurrection by being in relation with the world of the dead. Such a knowledge gained in the outside of society is similar to a non-knowledge.

For human beings, a "true" knowledge about the resurrection can only exist in society. This conclusion is consistent with the values of the first square of Interpretative Level II (cf. above, p. 83), which shows that the ideal believers (those who belong to the positive axis of the system of values of the gospel) care for others. How could they be attentive to (the needs of) others if under the pretense of believing in Jesus' resurrection they were to isolate themselves in an "outside of society" (an attitude which would demand that they turn themselves totally toward the transcendent)?

TOWARD A STUDY OF THE SYMBOLISM

The categories used in order to define the terms of the squares of the semantic universe presupposed by our text are nothing more than a first approximation. They now need to be defined more precisely with the help of the results of traditional exegesis. It should be clear that we have already made use of some of these results. As soon as we open a dictionary or a Greek grammar we are indebted to traditional exegesis. In the context of a critical discussion we would now need to integrate systematically the results of traditional exegesis with those of our structural exegesis. Through a detailed study of the text's symbolism, the categories used above could then be refined. Indeed, most of the textual elements concerning locations and time sequences, and also most of the things and personages referred to in the text, are associated with specific values. In what way do they contribute to the manifestation of these values? By which of their many semantic connotations? It is in the context of this study of symbolism that the parallel "narratives" of our text would also need to be considered, since they are nothing more than a series of symbols (none of these parallel narratives has a narrative development complete enough to manifest a system of pertinent transformations). The following remarks are intended merely as suggestions about the way in which a structural exegesis can contribute to the study of the symbolism of our text—a study that traditional exegesis has already developed from a historical perspective.

What does the "wine mingled with myrrh" (15:23) symbolize? The Catholic and Protestant biblical scholars who together prepared the recent *Traduction Oecuménique de la Bible* (Ecumenical Translation of the Bible) summarize in their notes some results of traditional exegesis on this point: "A Jewish practice which the Talmud bases on Proverbs 31:6, required that this drink which induces drowsiness, be given to those who are condemned." What do we learn from our structural exegesis? First that the refusal of the wine mingled with myrrh is made by the crucified Jesus who symbolizes the pertinent value /manifestation of one's volition while being powerless/. Jesus' submission is voluntary. In refusing to take this drink, Jesus refuses to be deprived from his volition; if he had lost consciousness—if he had become drowsy—he would not have manifested this value that characterizes the positive axis of the system of values of the gospel. In fact he would then belong to the negative axis together with the chief priests and the scribes. Thus in this case the re sults of traditional and structural exegesis are mutually supportive.

What does the "darkness over the whole land until the ninth hour" (15:33) symbolize? The translators of the *Traduction Oecuménique de la Bible* note: "This mention of the darkness at noon perhaps evokes the mourning of the only son according to Amos 8:9–10, cf. also Exodus 10:22." This symbol is associated both with "Jesus crucified," who represents a volition without power, and with "Jesus who saves others," who symbolizes a volition *and* a power for saving others (and negatively a non-volition for saving oneself despite one's power). It appears therefore that the darkness can be viewed as the manifestation of a cosmic power, a divine power. God could act in order to save his Chosen One. But he did not do so. This manifestation of divine power shows that God's inaction is itself voluntary. What is happening conforms to his will. Can we find similar connotations given to the symbol "darkness" in other (biblical, Jewish, Hellenistic) texts? Traditional exegesis has perhaps taken note of them without necessarily recognizing their pertinence here. The Old Testament texts quoted above are pertinent in that they use "darkness" as a symbol of the manifestation of God's cosmic power. Yet the emphasis is not upon the "mourning of the only son" as in Amos 8:9–10.

Considering now the reference to "the curtain of the temple torn in two from top to bottom" (15:38) we note first of all that it is juxtaposed to Jesus' uttering of a loud cry and then his expiration. We have seen (cf. the square of Interpretative Level III, p. 79) that this symbol represents "abandonment by God," in other words, the value /without God/. According to this correlation, the temple whose curtain is torn symbolizes a temple abandoned by God, that is, a temple that can no longer have its mediating role through which the distance separating God from man is overcome. These remarks are, as a whole, consistent with the results of traditional exegesis.

These brief remarks (which should be extended through a detailed comparative study of the semantic features of each symbol in our text and in other texts of the same cultural milieu) show that this type of research has the promise of opening up a fruitful dialogue between structural exegesis and traditional exegesis. We cannot perform such a study of the symbolism in this book, since our primary goal here is the development of a method of structural exegesis and the demonstration of its important hermeneutical implications. Some of these hermeneutical possibilities have already been suggested in the above study of the semantic universe presupposed by Mark 15 and 16. The contribution of structural exegesis, however, does not end here; it also permits the exegete to identify from among the many possible hermeneutics those which are legitimate.

Appendix to Chapter 3
NARRATIVE HIERARCHY OF MARK 15:43–46

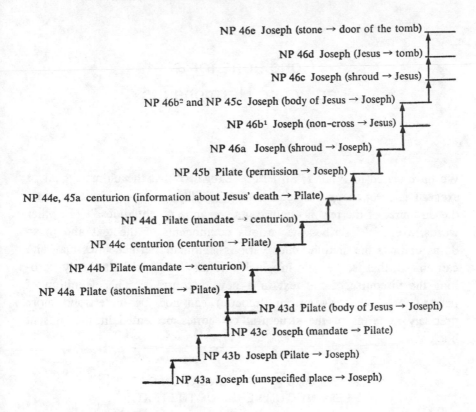

NP 46e Joseph (stone → door of the tomb)

NP 46d Joseph (Jesus → tomb)

NP 46c Joseph (shroud → Jesus)

NP 46b² and NP 45c Joseph (body of Jesus → Joseph)

NP 46b¹ Joseph (non-cross → Jesus)

NP 46a Joseph (shroud → Joseph)

NP 45b Pilate (permission → Joseph)

NP 44e, 45a centurion (information about Jesus' death → Pilate)

NP 44d Pilate (mandate → centurion)

NP 44c centurion (centurion → Pilate)

NP 44b Pilate (mandate → centurion)

NP 44a Pilate (astonishment → Pilate)

NP 43d Pilate (body of Jesus → Joseph)

NP 43c Joseph (mandate → Pilate)

NP 43b Joseph (Pilate → Joseph)

NP 43a Joseph (unspecified place → Joseph)

4

Conditions for a
Legitimate Hermeneutic

We have stated in *What Is Structural Exegesis?* that the ultimate goal of exegesis is to open up hermeneutical possibilities. "Exegesis determines the discourse of the text, its nature, its semantic potentialities."[1] In other words, exegesis describes the various components of the text and in so doing delimits the field in which various legitimate hermeneutics may and can unfold, that is, the field in which one may and can legitimately "prolong the discourse of the text in a new discourse." This definition of hermeneutic (taken over from Ricoeur) can now be understood more precisely in terms of the structural categories presented in the present book.

HERMENEUTIC AS PROLONGATION OF THE
SEMANTIC UNIVERSE OF THE TEXT

Mark 15 and 16 provide us with several examples of hermeneutic. Let us consider them. The passersby, the chief priests and scribes, and the robbers perform a hermeneutic upon an "event" that may be termed "acted-out discourse," that is, the crucifixion of Jesus by the soldiers; the bystanders (and the enunciator) perform a hermeneutic upon a spoken discourse, namely, Jesus' message; the centurion performs a hermeneutic upon an acted-out discourse, Jesus' expiration on the cross; the women perform a hermeneutic upon a twofold acted-out discourse, Jesus' expiration on the cross and Joseph's burying of Jesus; the young man performs a hermeneutic upon an acted-out discourse, that is, the women at the tomb. In each case the hermeneutic prolongs the "discourse," which is interpreted in a new "discourse." These hermeneutical discourses are themselves either acted-out discourses (cf. the bystanders and the women) or spoken discourses (the passersby, the chief priests and scribes, the robbers, the centurion, and the young man). The actions or words that

94

constitute their hermeneutical discourses are based upon a "knowledge" concerning either an event or a spoken discourse (belonging to the primary narrative level). Let us underscore this: it is an *interpretative* knowledge. It is not the mere knowledge about various facts (either the facts constituting the event or those related in the message) that leads the various characters to act or to speak but rather an interpretation of the *value* these facts have. This is clear in the centurion's case. He proclaims that Jesus is Son of God not merely because he is aware of the facts surrounding Jesus' death but because he recognizes in these facts a specific value that he expresses in his proclamation. The same is true in each of the other cases. The passersby, the chief priests and the scribes, and the robbers insult Jesus because they see in the fact that Jesus has been crucified a specific value—let us say, the value "false messiah." The bystanders who have heard Jesus' message act and speak as they do because they perceive in this message the value "call for help to Elijah" even though they do not understand the *signification* of this message (i.e., its informational or referential meaning). By contrast, the enunciator sees in this message the value "message without signification" (for the reader) and consequently gives a meaning to this message (his translation). The women go to the tomb after buying spices because they see in Joseph's action the value "burial without all the proper rites which Jesus as their Master should receive" (since they still see in the crucified Jesus the one they have been following). The young man addresses himself to the women as he does because he sees in them the value "fearful women who can be calmed down."

It is not possible to analyze in detail the interpretative processes involved in these different hermeneutics. The text does not describe them. Furthermore we only have an approximate knowledge of what has been interpreted even in the case of the interpretation of Jesus' message; the bystanders have interpreted both Jesus' words and the event that is the context within which this message has been uttered. Yet, for them, what is this event? How could we tell!? These bystanders interpret what they have seen and not Mark's story! The text does not tell us what they have seen. Thus we cannot study the hermeneutical process in this text. Yet we may note that a hermeneutic as prolongation of a discourse (whether acted out or spoken) into a new discourse (whether acted out or spoken) is based upon an interpretation of the *value* of the first discourse. The same holds true in the case of the interpretation of texts and of complete spoken discourses (i.e., of discourses with a signification), even though in this case the object to be interpreted already involves interpretation. Indeed, by contrast with an actual event (an acted-out discourse as series of events given without previous interpretation, or a message without signification as in 15:34a), a text or a discourse has a value by the very fact that it is set within the structural network of the phenomenon of human communication. Both somatic and discursive events are set forth along with the author's interpretation, which itself presupposes, among other things, a semantic universe.

What is the *value* of a discourse? In order to answer this question let us consider two examples provided by our text. The passersby, the chief priests and the scribes, and the robbers interpret the event "crucified Jesus" in terms of a set of categories (which are not specified) according to which the event "crucified Jesus" has a negative value. By contrast, the centurion interprets the same event in terms of categories according to which the event "crucified Jesus" has a positive value. In other words, these two hermeneutics have been carried out in terms of two different isotopies that belong, insofar as we can tell, to two (or more, in view of the number of personages involved) different idiolectal semantic universes. Thus we can conclude that the new discourse (the hermeneutical discourse) is based upon an interpretation of the original discourse in terms of a specific semantic universe. If indeed a (legitimate) hermeneutic is the *prolongation* of a discourse into a new discourse, we can say that this new discourse is based upon the *interpretation of the original discourse in terms of an isotopy that is compatible with one or several of its isotopies.*

Thus it appears that the hermeneutical prolongation of the discourse of a text is not so much the prolongation of the logic of the narrative (or discursive) development as it is the prolongation of its semantic universe. The hermeneutic, as interpretative process, interrupts the formal narrative development in order to introduce a new narrative level manifesting a new semantic universe which is interrelated with that of the text in the same way as the isotopies of the interpretative levels of Mark 15 and 16 are interrelated with the isotopy of the primary level.

On the basis of the preceding discussion we identify two issues regarding the nature of the hermeneutical process which demand a more complete treatment.

(1) A legitimate hermeneutic is based upon the hermeneut's appropriation of at least one part of the semantic universe of the original discourse. In this way the hermeneut's semantic universe and the text's semantic universe can eventually be interrelated. We will need to address the question: How does this appropriation take place?

(2) In most instances the new discourse does not presuppose the same semantic universe as the original discourse. The hermeneutical discourse has its own semantic universe, even though it is interrelated with that of the original discourse. We must address the following questions: How do these two different semantic universes become interrelated? What types of relations can exist between the two semantic universes?

We shall begin by a discussion of the latter set of questions, which will allow us to propose a distinction between two types of hermeneutic.

TWO TYPES OF HERMENEUTIC

Two types of relations can exist between the semantic universe of the hermeneutical discourse and the semantic universe of the text.

In a hermeneutic of the first sort, the semantic universe of the new discourse can be interrelated with the universe of the text in such a way that the first contributes, in its own way, to the "mythical" (cf. Lévi-Strauss) demonstration that an opposition of the semantic universe of the text receives a mediation. In this case the hermeneutical discourse proposes a new series of mediated oppositions (and hence a new series of squares) that prolongs the demonstration of the validity of the semantic universe of the text in the hermeneut's discourse (and life). These new mediated oppositions (which are secondary oppositions as compared with the more fundamental oppositions of the semantic universe of the text) in this way establish the semantic universe of the text as the universe that the hermeneut accepts as his own. He incorporates his discourse and life into this semantic universe. In this first case the hermeneut's new discourse and life are embedded in the semantic universe of the text, the value of which is thus absolutized. It is clear that this type of hermeneutic is characteristic of the hermeneutic of sacred texts, that is, of texts that present themselves as manifesting certain revelations (revelations being the most fundamental values of a semantic universe). This is why we shall refer to this type of hermeneutic as *sacred hermeneutic,* that is, the hermeneutic viewing the text as sacred. Yet we cannot rule out the possibility that such a hermeneutic may be performed on profane texts as well (that is, upon texts which present themselves as manifesting secondary values but which are nevertheless viewed as if they were sacred texts).

In a second type of hermeneutic, *profane hermeneutic,* that is, a hermeneutic viewing the text as profane, the relations between the semantic universe of the new discourse with the universe of the text are inverted. The text is interpreted in such a way that it demonstrates the validity of the system of values of the hermeneutical discourse which prolongs it. In other words, the semantic universe of the text (the oppositions of which are viewed as secondary) is interrelated with the semantic universe of the hermeneutical discourse (the oppositions of which are viewed as more fundamental) in such a way that it is the validity of the latter which is mythically established. The hermeneut's discourse (and life) and the semantic universe that it presupposes are thus justified by the text. This type of hermeneutic is characteristic of the hermeneutic of profane texts, that is, of texts that presuppose oppositions which are secondary as compared with the oppositions of the hermeneutical discourse. Yet, it can also be used in the interpretation of sacred texts—which then are no longer viewed as having the character of absolute revelation.

Before considering examples of both types of hermeneutic, we need to establish the criteria that will allow us to discern those instances when each type of hermeneutic is legitimate. These two types of hermeneutic are very different, and the choice of one or the other will have many implications; therefore it is crucial that we be in a position to control this choice.

FIRST CRITERION OF LEGITIMACY:
SACRED TEXT VS. PROFANE TEXT

In the following discussion we shall presuppose that a hermeneutic is legitimate only insofar as it respects the character of the interpreted text. Such a statement needs no validation; to interpret a book of traffic regulations as if it were poetry would be to perform an illegitimate hermeneutic. This statement implies, therefore, that a hermeneutic is legitimate if and only if it interprets as "sacred" that text which presents itself as a "sacred" text and as "profane" that text which presents itself as a "profane" text. We are then faced with this question: Is it possible to make a formal distinction between a "sacred" and a "profane" text? In other words, is it possible to distinguish formally a text whose semantic universe needs to be mythically established and demonstrated by its legitimate hermeneutic (the case of a "sacred" text) from a text that is used by its legitimate hermeneutic as the mythical demonstration of the validity of the semantic universe characterizing the hermeneutical discourses (the case of a "profane" text)?

As noted above, the semantic universe of the hermeneutical discourse is interrelated with that of the text in the same way as the isotopies of the interpretative narrative levels are interrelated with the isotopy of the primary narrative level. In other words, the hermeneutical discourse can be viewed as an additional interpretative narrative level,[2] and conversely the interpretative narrative levels can be viewed as hermeneutical discourses prolonging the primary level of the text. Since a hermeneutic is the "prolongation" of the discourse of the text at the semantic level, we can conclude that the relations between the semantic universe of a text and the semantic universe of the hermeneutical discourse which prolongs it should be the same as the relations that exist in the text between the isotopy of the primary level and the isotopies of the interpretative levels. If the primary level presupposes a set of semantic categories that are more fundamental than those of the interpretative levels, then the text is a *sacred* text. In order to be legitimate, its hermeneutic should be of the first type. By contrast, if the primary level of the text presupposes a set of semantic categories that are *less* fundamental than those of the interpretative levels, the text is a *profane*[3] text. In order to be legitimate, its hermeneutic should then be of the second type.

Thus, in order to establish formally whether a text presents itself as "sacred" or "profane," it is necessary to compare the values manifested by its various narrative levels so as to determine where the most fundamental values are manifested. For the time being the identification of the most fundamental values can only be made in terms of their semantic proximity to the values involved in the existential opposition "life vs. death" (or "God vs. man"). Such a procedure is usually adequate. However, we hope that more formal criteria will be established in the future.

MARK 15 AND 16 AS "PROFANE" TEXT

Is Mark 15 and 16 a "profane" or a "sacred" text? To answer this question let us consider the semantic categories found in the isotopies of the primary and interpretative levels. It is clear that the semantic categories presupposed by the interpretative levels are more fundamental than those presupposed by the primary level. The isotopy of Interpretative Level III actually includes the opposition "God vs. man." The isotopy of Interpretative Level I deals with the relations between human society and manifestations of the transcendent. By contrast, at the primary narrative level we find a modal isotopy, that is, an isotopy concerning various attitudes which are less fundamental in that they presuppose a specific order of society and the world in its relation to God. On the basis of these observations we must conclude that our text presents itself as a "profane" text and *not* as a "sacred" text. Exegetes and theologians who are aware of the iconoclastic character of parts of the biblical texts should not be surprised by this conclusion. We can expect that this conclusion will apply to the whole Gospel (as the study of other passages suggests), but so far it has only been demonstrated in the case of Mark 15 and 16.

As a consequence of the "profane" character of Mark 15 and 16, a legitimate hermeneutic will need to be such that the Gospel text be used to confirm the validity of the more fundamental values presupposed by our (spoken or acted-out) discourses that prolong the discourse of the text. It is within our experience as told (or retold) by our discourses and within our lives that the most fundamental values of our semantic universe (the mediated oppositions "life vs. death" and "God vs. man") should be discovered. In other words, it is *in our present experience* (and not in the text of the Gospel) that we are to discover a meaning for our life and the presence of God. Yet in order to have such a hermeneutic it is also necessary that the hermeneutical discourse which presupposes this twofold discovery be such that its semantic universe and the semantic universe of the text be interrelated with each other (as the isotopies of the text are interrelated with each other) so as to form a complex semantic universe.

SECOND CRITERION OF LEGITIMACY:
HERMENEUTIC AND THE APPROPRIATION OF THE
SEMANTIC UNIVERSE OF THE TEXT

The semantic universe of the hermeneut and that of the text must be "compatible" with one another in order to be interrelated to form a complex semantic universe. In many cases (or should we say, in most cases?) this means that one of the two must be modified to match the other. Whether the textual discourse or the hermeneutical discourse manifests the more fundamental categories, *a hermeneutic can be viewed as legitimate[4] only when it respects the integrity of the text's semantic universe.* Thus, a legitimate hermeneutic demands that we as hermeneuts agree to modify our own semantic universes so as to adapt them to the text's universe. Such an attitude presupposes that we view the text's system of values as "truer" than our own. In other words, the hermeneut must view this text as having the authority (the value) of "canon." Let us underscore this. Any text can function as a "canon." A "profane" text as well as a "sacred" text functions as "canon" when its semantic integrity is respected by the hermeneutic. For the hermeneut this text is "canon" (or Scripture). Thus, a legitimate hermeneutic demands that as hermeneuts we first appropriate for ourselves the text's semantic universe in such a way that this universe becomes a part of the complex semantic universe presupposed in our new discourse. Let us now consider the dynamics of this *appropria-tion*—the first stage of the hermeneutical process.

IDEA VS. DEEP VALUE

Let us note the nature of the object that is to be appropriated: the semantic universe presupposed by the text. It is not a system of "ideas" (in the common sense of the term: "any representation elaborated by thought") but rather a system of deep values presupposed by conscious intellectual activity (and, hence, not established by it). These deep values are "self-evident." They are truths that impose themselves upon us with such power that no further proof is needed in order to perceive their validity and reality. This implies that these deep values *cannot* be communicated in the same way ideas are communicated.

In order to transmit an idea, one establishes it by means of an argument that provides a series of proofs. If the logic and the validity of this argu-ment are accepted, the idea is received.[5] This cannot be the process through which deep values are transmitted. If they were demonstrated by a logical argument they would be no longer "*self-evident* truths" but rather "dem-onstrated truths"! In losing their self-evidence they would also lose the ability, the power, to function as "the conditions of possibility of a dis-course"[6] (which they have as elements of a semantic universe). When an idea is introduced in a discourse it is manifested by a word (or by a more complex discursive unit), that is, by a sign (or several signs). The idea as cognitive sign participates in the syntagmatic development of the dis-course in that, as with any sign, it refers to both the idea itself and (either implicitly or explicitly) to the series of proofs which have established it in a discursive development. In the same way, a somatic sign refers to a concrete situation *and* to the series of events that have established it in a narrative development. Thus the idea as sign is characterized by the rela-tion between signifier and signified (as referential dimension of the sign). These two elements can be differentiated because their relationship is arbitrary and variable; the same signifier can refer to different signifieds. Because a distance separates these two elements, the sign can be manipu-lated by the intellectual activity that governs the (syntagmatic) logic of any discourse.[7]

Therefore an idea is manifested by a sign (or by a series of signs). By contrast, a deep value cannot be directly manifested by a sign. As a self-evident truth it cannot refer to an entity established by the logic of a syn-tagmatic development (whether discursive or narrative). A deep value is an "immediate" truth that as such cannot tolerate the distance separating signifier from signified. We could say that it refers to nothing other than itself, that it is a "pure signified," or even an "opaque sign," that is, a "defective sign," where all distinctions between signifier and signified are abolished. In other words, a deep value cannot be directly manifested by a normal sign. It can only be manifested symbolically, that is, paradigmatically. Instead of being manifested by a sign (as is an idea) it is manifested by the relations that exist *between* the signs of a given system. Because of its self-evidence and immediacy, a deep value has the power to impose itself upon a person apart from conscious intellectual activity. Such activity cannot manipulate a deep value because, in its case, there is no distance comparable to that which exists in the sign between signifier and signified. However, because of its power, a deep value (as an element of a semantic universe) establishes the meaningful context apart from which intellectual activity could not take place, since it would be without foundation.

DEEP VALUES AND RELIGIOUS CONVICTIONS

These deep values may also be described in terms of the religious phenomenon. Note first that what was just said about a deep value could as well be said of an idol. One constructs an idol when one identifies the symbol for the divine with the divine itself, that is, when signifier and signified are no longer distinguished from one another.[8] Even though it is a false god (that which is not god being considered as god), the idol nevertheless has actual power over the believer. It charms him, casts a spell upon him, and so imposes itself upon him. This power of the idol and the beliefs associated with it is none other than the power of deep values.

These last remarks concerning idols apply as well to the true God and his revelations. A revelation is nothing other than a self-evident truth; its sole "proof" rests with the One to whom it refers. It imposes itself upon the believer as a transcendent truth and not as the result of logical reasoning. It has the amazing power to transform one's life by providing a specific vision of the human experience and of the world. Thus a religious conviction is what we have called a "deep value."

THE APPROPRIATION OF RELIGIOUS CONVICTIONS

History of religion (also known as phenomenology of religion) has shown in which ways religious convictions are transmitted (a question that must not be confused with that of the origin of these convictions). Let us consider some of the conclusions reached through this research.

Religious convictions are not transmitted by means of logical arguments; they are not ideas (theological reflection is a second-order phenomenon) but self-evident truths.[9] Consequently, they are communicated indirectly through the intermediary of rituals and sacred stories, myths or scriptures. Let us consider the case of a mythical religion. In a ritual the believers do not read myths objectively but rather retell them, reenact them, incarnate them, live them. In so doing, either the believers "enter" into the mythical story, by projecting themselves upon (or into) the mythical story, or they integrate the mythical story within their own history, by projecting the mythical story into their own history. In either case the semantic universe presupposed by the mythical story becomes a part of the believers' semantic universe. This is readily seen in the first instance. By "entering" into the text, the believers "enter" into the semantic universe presupposed by the text; their own semantic universe is thus subordinated to that of the text. The same is true in the second instance, though the movement is reversed. In both cases the believers, as a result of their participation in the ritual, gain a semantic universe that is more complex and richer than the original one. The deep values presupposed by the mythical story have been transmitted to them as deep values.

The ritual provides us with a model of the process through which the appropriation of the semantic universe presupposed by a text takes place. It is clear that this first stage of the hermeneutic can be found in many other contexts. It takes place whenever the reader is so passionately involved in his reading that he "lives" the text, because in this case also the text's story becomes his own story. The appropriation of a text's semantic universe is therefore an indirect process which requires that the story of the text be interrelated with the hermeneut's "story" (or history), or at least with a portion of it. This process will take place in different ways, according to the character of the text.

THE HERMENEUTIC OF A "SACRED" TEXT

When the text is considered "sacred"—that is, a complete and final revelation—the hermeneut identifies his story with the text's. His story is only a "variant" of the text's story. The most classical example of this type of hermeneutic is seen in the Jewish Passover. In order to celebrate this feast the believers retell the history of the Exodus as if it were their own history: "*We* went out of Egypt . . ." This identification implies that the believers (be they individuals or a community) can assimilate at least a part of their experience to a part of the narrative. Consequently, the semantic universe of the sacred text becomes their own semantic universe. They can then recognize themselves as the Chosen People (rather than as a people like other peoples).

A theological discourse may eventually express this hermeneutical process by asserting that the revealed identity of the Jewish community as the Chosen People (a series of fundamental values) has been revealed once and for all on Mount Sinai (i.e., through the establishment of the covenant in the time of the Exodus). Thus, from the standpoint of the theological discourse the sacred text proves the validity of the semantic universe presupposed by the present Jewish community. By contrast, from the standpoint of the symbolic logic of the mythical system the very existence of such a Jewish community is proof of the validity of the text's semantic universe. The fact that in the present situation a people recognizes itself as the Chosen People and lives as such is the symbolic assertion of the eternal covenant revealed in Scripture.

In the case of the hermeneutic of a sacred text, the hermeneutical process begins with a "retelling" of the text that can take various forms (according to the type of experiences and situations brought to the text by the hermeneut). This is the appropriation stage that, in the Jewish literature, is termed the Haggadah. In a second stage of the hermeneutic a new discourse (either spoken or acted-out) is developed. This new discourse presupposes this revelation of fundamental values and manifests their implications for various aspects of human experience. In the example of Pharisaic Judaism, these new discourses are often ethical discourses, a halakah, the way to walk which should be followed by the Chosen People in the concrete cultural situations of its daily life.[10] In such a case the structural exegesis of both the sacred text and the hermeneutical discourse would provide a means of verifying the validity of the ethics derived from the sacred text.

A hermeneutic of this type upon Mark 15 and 16 would be illegitimate, because this text presents itself as a "profane" text. Since our text is nevertheless frequently taken as a "sacred" text (because it is read together with the Gospel of Matthew which, according to a number of preliminary studies, appears to manifest the more fundamental values at the primary narrative level), it might be useful to illustrate briefly what such a hermeneutic would be like even though our exegesis shows it to be illegitimate.

On the basis of the values of Interpretative Level III, Jesus is viewed as the complete and final mediation of the opposition "God vs. man." To believe in Jesus is to believe that in him the separation between God and man is once and for all overcome. Jesus is also the "ideal man" (he is a man not separated from God); he is the Son of God. In following him, by identifying oneself with him, one also becomes an "ideal man" and "son of God." Thus, being a disciple is being a true ("real") person who actualizes within himself the fullness of what it means to be human. It is "not being separated from God" and, therefore, having a true meaning and purpose for one's life. Thus, one "retells" the story of the Gospel by identifying oneself with the SUBJECTS[11] of the positive axis. One projects upon the text one's life and experience. Consequently, one assumes the identity of "disciple," of "son of God." This is the appropriation stage that takes place in religious services and in meditation upon Scripture. Yet, beyond this one must also live, think, and speak as a disciple. For this purpose one strives to live as Jesus and the other SUBJECTS of the positive axis did (Jesus and these SUBJECTS are viewed as models to be emulated).

One strives to ignore the accusations made by other people and to remain silent. One avoids bringing accusations against another out of jealousy and allowing oneself to be carried away by the excitement linked with the leveling of such accusations. One strives to submit to the other person's will and to avoid using one's own power over others and to do this willingly since one is striving to live in the hope of true deliverance rather than in the illusion of human deliverances. One strives to be respectful vis-à-vis the political authority, while recognizing that the ultimate authority is the true religious authority manifested in Jesus. One strives to live for others (as Jesus did) and to be attentive to others (as the centurion was) and one avoids living for oneself. One strives to have a religious attitude (to approach the transcendent) and one professes to be waiting for the intervention of the transcendent in one's life and in society. One strives to believe in the resurrection, that is, to believe that the crucified Jesus was resurrected (or was risen from the dead). Is this not the ultimate confirmation that he is indeed the One who, once and for all, has reestablished (or established) the possibility of a harmonious (just) relationship between God and man?

When manifested in the religious and daily life of the believer, such a hermeneutic is admirable—as was the case with the hermeneutic of the faithful Pharisee. It seems to be a legitimate hermeneutic of the Gospel of Matthew. Yet it is an illegitimate hermeneutic of the Gospel of Mark, since it involves interpreting a "profane" text as if it were a "sacred" text.

THE HERMENEUTIC OF A "PROFANE" TEXT

The legitimate hermeneutic of a "profane" text views the text as "canon" in the same way as the hermeneutic of a "sacred" text does. Thus its first stage is also an appropriation of the text's semantic universe, even though the appropriation process is the reverse of what it was in the preceding case; it involves the projection of the text upon the hermeneut's story rather than the projection of the hermeneut's story upon the text.

An example of such a hermeneutic is also to be found in early Judaism: the Apocalyptic hermeneutic.[12] The biblical text is no longer viewed as complete and final revelation but as "types"[13] and "promises" that are fulfilled (at least in part) in the hermeneut's present. In the events around them the apocalyptists expected to discover God at work, that is, the fulfillment of certain of these promises and types. The biblical text was therefore used as the key that provided access to the meaning of contemporary events. The events which, from the hermeneuts' standpoint, were viewed as analogous to the positive events of the biblical narrative (the types) were recognized as acts of God. The acts of God in the past sacred history were revelations, the revelations of covenants through which God called a people or a person (election) to be his Chosen for specific tasks (vocations). Similarly, the new acts of God were new revelations (new *fundamental values*) through which the hermeneuts discovered their true identity as chosen for a specific vocation. Thus, by means of such a hermeneutic the apocalyptists discovered the fundamental values that gave meaning and authenticity to their lives *in the events of their contemporary history* and not in the biblical text or in the biblical events. Yet the biblical text was the "canon" through which they could discover the meaning of those contemporary events. As already noted, it was the events that were discovered to be analogous to the positive elements of the text which were recognized as manifestations of God in history. By contrast, the events that were viewed as being analogous to elements of the text's negative axis were recognized as being manifestations of an anti-election and an anti-vocation that, if accepted, would condemn the apocalyptists to perdition, to unauthenticity, and to a life without true meaning.

Within such a hermeneutic the appropriation stage is therefore a "retelling," a reinterpretation, a new vision, of the hermeneuts' present story (or history) in terms of the biblical text's categories. The hermeneuts (as either individuals or group) discover in events around them fundamental values: their election and their vocation. In a second stage the hermeneutic unfolds in a life (i.e., a discourse both acted out and spoken) based upon these fundamental values; the hermeneuts carry out their vocation. Here also the biblical text provides various models (as it does in the case of the hermeneutic of "sacred" texts), yet the hermeneuts are not bound by these models; they must first satisfy the demands of their new election and of their new vocation.[14]

The dangers in such a hermeneutic are clear when we consider the excesses it has engendered. Since the most fundamental values belong to the hermeneutical discourse and not to the biblical text, the hermeneut easily betrays the text. The integrity of its semantic universe is no longer respected. Furthermore, this hermeneutic involves a constant change in fundamental values attuned to the rhythm of the ever-changing experiences "retold" in the hermeneutical discourses. In order to control its legitimacy, one cannot any longer call upon an institution whose role would be to maintain stable fundamental values (expressed in the form of orthodox doctrines). Yet it is this type of hermeneutic that our text requires because of the organization of its semantic universe. Structural exegesis provides a means for verifying the legitimacy of such hermeneutics.

A hermeneutic of Mark 15 and 16, which is a "profane" text, must begin by an appropriation of its semantic universe through the contemplation of our experience and of the events of our present in light of the text. For this purpose we should not bracket out what characterizes our experience so as better to identify ourselves with the narrative, but we should on the contrary search our experience so as to discover which of its elements in their specificity may be viewed as analogous to those of the text. It is a matter not of transcending the specificity of our experience in order to enter into the specifics of the text but of transcending the specifics of the text so as to apply it to our experience. The narrative and symbolic manifestation of the text will be viewed as an invitation to "read" our experience in such a way that it might be perceived as a story which manifests the most fundamental values of a semantic universe coherent with the universe of the text. In other words, the text is a promise or a type that orients the reader's "gaze"[15] toward a "beyond" of the text—the reader's experience—in which God will eventually be discovered at work. This promise—or type—will be viewed as fulfilled when we as readers discover in our own experiences events that can be "retold" in such a way as to manifest the same system of deep values as the text. The hermeneutical discourse is, therefore, in a first stage a "retelling" of the hermeneut's experience.

Within our family life, the church, the social life around us, our work, the political world, we, as hermeneuts, will certainly discover those situations in which certain values presupposed by the text (and especially the less fundamental values) play a role. We might discover people making accusations against other people on account of jealousy. We might read a story in a newspaper that manifests an excitement related to such accusations. We might see someone submitting himself to the will of others, and so on, with each of the values presupposed by our text. Thus we are invited by the biblical text to discover the elements of our experience that "correspond" to elements of the story about Jesus, Pilate, the chief priests, the crowd, the soldiers, the centurion, Joseph, the women, and the young man. Yet, it is a matter of finding within our experience not a story about a crucifixion or a death sentence but stories that involve (whatever the personages and the performances) the values of one or more of the squares of the text's semantic universe.

In most instances these events from the hermeneut's experience have already been interpreted according to another system of values; a system that is presupposed by his culture. For example, these events might have been interpreted in terms of a system of values that characterizes the political world or the hierarchical relations at work or a religious institution or family relations. Consequently, each of these events is perceived—either explicitly or implicitly—as forming a narrative (or a part of one) that presupposes one of these systems of values.

In certain cases some of the values presupposed by the biblical text are both manifested and pertinent in this cultural narrative, but they do not have the same place within the system of values; they are on the other semantic axis (e.g., submission to another person's will is viewed as being negative) or correlated with different values (e.g., submission is correlated with a lack of will rather than with a voluntary refusal to use one's power on one's own behalf).

In other cases (in most instances) some of the values presupposed by the biblical text are to be found in the cultural story, but they are not pertinent values; the cultural story is not organized in terms of these values. The hermeneutic of Mark 15 and 16 will integrate these elements from the hermeneut's experience into a new story in such a way as to attribute to each the place it must have according to the text's system of values.

This transformation of the system of values presupposed by the culture is accomplished indirectly, namely, by transforming the narrative manifestation. The hermeneuts must retell these events in a new way, that is, in terms of the values of the biblical text. They identify one (or more) personage(s) from their own experience with Jesus; others they identify with Pilate, the soldiers, the crowd, and so on.[16] Yet let us stress that these identifications must be made in terms of the pertinent values of our text. For instance, the personages who manifest a non-imposition of their will upon others, a submission to the will of others (and this not out of a lack of will but because of their refusal to use their power upon others), who live for others and not for themselves, who sustain their relation with God even though they know that they are abandoned by God, such personages will be identified with Jesus. The same would be true for each of the personages who manifest one or several pertinent values. These identifications may exceptionally be complete identifications of a contemporary personage manifesting all the values displayed by a personage of the biblical text. Yet, in most instances, only partial identification will be found; a contemporary personage may manifest only one (or only a few) of the values manifested by a biblical personage. This is a reminder that in the hermeneutical process the "personage" is *not* a pertinent unit (a point that we have emphasized constantly following those structuralist scholars specializing in narrative studies). Thus the values manifested by a single personage in the biblical story may be manifested by several personages in the hermeneutical discourse, and vice versa.

Let us also note that this hermeneutical process may take place even though the contemporary events manifest only a few values of the text's semantic universe; for instance, two of the values of one square. In such a circumstance, when the story of these contemporary events is "retold" it may be complemented by envisioning hypothetical elements (e.g., by describing what could have happened). This way of proceeding to the retelling of events, which allows the speaker to establish certain pertinent oppositions, is quite commonly used in narratives. Such is the case in Mark 15:31–32, where we find the description by the chief priests of what they would do if Jesus would save himself by climbing down from the cross.

Through this first stage of the hermeneutic of the text (appropriation of its semantic universe) we as hermeneuts acquire a new vision of the situation, of the events, and of the persons around us. In some elements of our experience, we see manifestations of negative values that characterize the Gospel story. Since, as noted in the preceding chapter, the Gospel's semantic universe is often opposed to the semantic universes of our societies, these manifestations of the negative values are readily identifiable. This identification of the negative values already shows the pertinence of the gospel system of values; it is applicable to our experience! If we have discovered manifestations of the negative values, we can also expect to discover among the events around us manifestations of the positive values of the gospel narrative—or at least of some of them—even though we might have to look at our experience more carefully because we are not used to seeing it in this way.

Discovering some manifestations of the positive values, the hermeneut following Mark 15 and 16 can then declare with the centurion: truly, this man is Son of God; or, truly, in this person the gospel is manifested. These events, these persons, these situations manifest for him the fundamental values upon which he can now build a life that will be truly meaningful.

For the hermeneut these events are revelation. He is called to "follow" the way opened by them. In so doing he will follow not human beings (these manifest the gospel only in some aspects of their lives) but the manifestation of the gospel in them. Better still, the hermeneut will follow the manifestation of Christ in them—this Christ for whom he should look not outside of society (past history is an outside of society as well as the tomb) but in society where he precedes them. Thus each hermeneut becomes a "disciple." This term, however, should not be understood in the sense it would have in a hermeneutic viewing the text as "sacred." Here the hermeneut is not called upon to strive to make his life the incarnation in a new situation of the model represented by Jesus and the other positive personages of the biblical text. This would be to make of the gospel a law comparable to the Law that the Pharisees strove to fulfill. This would be to hope that by following this model one could make a "disciple" out of oneself and, thus, that through one's life one could manifest the gospel, the presence of Christ and of God in the world. On the contrary, the hermeneut discovers the gospel manifested in the world, the Christ at work in society, the transcendent intervening in human history, even before the hermeneut does anything. His spoken hermeneutical discourse will proclaim the news of this discovery. His acted-out hermeneutical discourse will simply follow what is already in progress. Confronted with the active presence of Christ, he is called upon to serve him. It is a matter not of doing again what is discovered as already taking place but rather of joining in the action, of helping and facilitating its development. Following this discovery his life will prolong the semantic universe of the gospel story.

From the above remarks it appears that the text opens up a multitude of possible legitimate hermeneutics. A given hermeneut will perform a new hermeneutic each time his or her new experiences are reread in the light of the text. Various hermeneuts will prolong the discourse of the text in the direction of various experiences. The Gospel text (as with any text) offers itself as "the conditions of possibility" of a quasi-infinity of (acted out or spoken) discourses. This is to say that there is no normative hermeneutic. This is why we do not provide an example of the hermeneutic of Mark 15 and 16; it would appear as a norm! Let the reader perform his own hermeneutic! This will be the best demonstration that structural exegesis actually opens up hermeneutical possibilities.

It should be clear that such a hermeneutic can take place without a prior structural exegesis of the text. The role of such an exegesis is to provide a means of control. For the reader, for the believer, it is simply a matter of perceiving his experience in the light of the text. This series of identifications takes place more or less spontaneously when the believer perceives the text to be a "canon" (or "Scripture") and receives the text as a series of "types" and promises that are fulfilled in the present. In other words, the first stage of the profane hermeneutic—which can also be termed a prophetic interpretation—requires that the believer have a faith according to which this biblical text is Scripture (word of God) as a "profane" text (that is, as a text which does *not* manifest a complete and final revelation).

The dangers of such a prophetic interpretation are well known. Jewish apocalyptic literature as well as various Christian "prophetic" movements (movements that involve either Christians exulting in spiritual charisma or Christians overflowing with political zeal) have provided throughout the centuries many examples of illegitimate hermeneutics in addition to numerous legitimate hermeneutics. The text is often nothing more than a pretext for justifying a way of looking at the events of one's experience which has been established on the basis of another semantic universe (e.g., an ideology, a religious belief). Whatever the terminology employed, the believer and his friends are "Jesus"-like or "centurion"-like people and their enemies are Pilate-like, soldiers-like, or chief priests-like people. Thus, the text does not teach anything to the believers. It does not challenge their way of seeing what is around them. Consequently, being afraid of falling into the trap of this kind of illegitimate hermeneutic, one refuses to engage oneself in any prophetic hermeneutic—even in the case where the text (such as Mark 15 and 16) offers itself as a "profane" text. If one does not relegate the text to dusty archives (which might be of interest to the scholar but not to oneself), one strives to make a less dangerous (albeit illegitimate) hermeneutic by considering this text as "sacred." For instance, the hermeneutical discourse finds in the text a moral teaching. In so doing, one has lost any possibility of discovering what the text promises: the one who precedes us in our society.

As a means for controlling the legitimacy of the hermeneutic of a text, structural exegesis reopens the possibility of profane (or prophetic) hermeneutics. The believers need not be afraid of being trapped into wild or fanatic illegitimate prophetic interpretations; the text rigorously delimits the field in which its various legitimate hermeneutics may unfold, and a structural exegesis of this text shows what this field is. The dangers involved in prophetic interpretations are warded off by viewing the text as the "canon" against which any of its hermeneutics should be measured. Indeed, as a consequence of structural exegesis that elucidates the semantic universe presupposed by the biblical text, this text can then fulfill its function as "canon," as Scripture.

A structural exegesis shows whether a specific biblical text must be viewed as an open canon (as in the case of our text) or as a closed canon. In order to be legitimate, a hermeneutic of this text must be, respectively, either a sacred hermeneutic or a profane (prophetic) hermeneutic. In either case many different hermeneutics of the same text are possible, since each hermeneut will retell his or her own experience in terms of the text. Yet in order to be legitimate these hermeneutics need to be properly related to the semantic universe of the text; the legitimacy or illegitimacy of any given hermeneutic can be demonstrated by comparing the semantic universe of the hermeneutical discourse with that of the text.

In the case of a "profane" text, such as Mark 15 and 16, one can then take the risk of following the fluctuation of prophetic hermeneutics. One is no longer paralyzed by the fear of being trapped into an illegitimate hermeneutic. Looking around, one can then boldly make an apparently foolish confession of faith: truly, this person is the Son of God.

Notes

CHAPTER 1

1. D. Patte, *What Is Structural Exegesis?* (Philadelphia: Fortress Press, 1976).

2. I allude to what Foucault would call a "gaze" (French, *regard*). The various types of structuralist research manifest the emergence of a new "gaze" upon the phenomenon of a "meaningful text." For more on the concept of "gaze" see M. Foucault, *The Birth of the Clinic* (New York: Vintage Books, 1973).

3. Cf. Patte, *What Is Structural Exegesis?* chap. 2.

4. As I suggested earlier this new perception of "meaning" results from a wider shift in preunderstandings that affects our culture as a whole. Structuralist research is merely one manifestation of this shift. Cf. ibid., chap. 1.

5. Cf. Robert C. Tannehill, *The Sword of His Mouth* (Philadelphia: Fortress Press, 1975), pp. 1–37.

6. Cf. ibid., p. 18. Tannehill quotes this phrase from Krieger, *The Play and Place of Criticism* (Baltimore: Johns Hopkins, 1967). In its original context this phrase refers to "rhetoric," a type of "plain speech."

7. Ibid., p. 11. Tannehill refers to Philip Wheelwright, *The Burning Fountain*, rev. ed. (Bloomington: Indiana University Press, 1968), pp. 86–88.

8. Tannehill, *The Sword of His Mouth*, p. 19 and passim.

9. Tannehill might agree with this statement since he notes that the synoptic sayings are on the borderline between rhetoric (a type of informational language) and poetry (symbolic language). Ibid., p. 18.

10. P. Tillich, *The Dynamics of Faith* (New York: Harper & Row, 1957).

11. This is true whether we subordinate our own vision to that of the text or vice versa.

12. M. Foucault, *The Birth of the Clinic,* pp. ix–xix.

13. M. Foucault, *La Volonté de Savoir* (Paris: Gallimard, 1977).

14. M. Foucault, *The Order of Things* (New York: Pantheon Books, 1970); *Archeology of Knowledge* (New York: Vintage Books, 1973); and *The Birth of the Clinic.*

15. This lecture was delivered January 7, 1977. Most of the text of this lecture was published in *Le Monde* (Paris, January 10, 1977).

16. Cf. Patte, *What Is Structural Exegesis?* chap. 2, on the concept of "value" as developed by F. de Saussure.

17. A. J. Greimas, *Maupassant: La Sémiotique du Texte* (Paris: Seuil, 1976). It is a 250-page analysis of a short story by Maupassant.

18. I.e., a system of values that is the axis around which the text is organized.

19. F. Streng, *Understanding Religious Life,* 2d ed. (Encino, Calif.: Dickenson, 1976), p. 7.

20. Ibid., p. 8.

21. Ibid., p. 9.

22. Ibid., p. 86.

23. C. Loew, *Myth, Sacred History, and Philosophy* (New York: Harcourt, Brace and World, 1967), pp. 3ff.

24. Tannehill (following Ray Hart, *Unfinished Man and the Imagination* [New York: Herder and Herder, 1968]) points out from a different perspective the close relationship between the "forceful and imaginative language" and "revelation." Tannehill, *The Sword of His Mouth,* pp. 21–28.

25. Cf. Patte, *What Is Structural Exegesis?* chap. 2.

26. Cf. ibid.

27. R. Barthes, *S/Z* (Paris: Seuil, 1970).

28. A. J. Greimas, *Sémiotique et Sciences Sociales* (Paris: Seuil, 1976).

29. P. Geoltrain, "La violation du Sabbat: Une lecture de Marc 3:1–6," *Cahiers Bibliques* 9 (1970): 70–90; and "Les Noces de Cana: Jean 2:1–11," *Foie et Vie,* no. 13 (1974): 83–90.

30. J. Calloud, *Structural Analysis of Narrative,* trans. D. Patte (Philadelphia: Fortress Press, 1976).

31. J. Delorme is editor of *Signes et Paraboles* (Paris: Seuil, 1977), which includes essays by A. J. Greimas and J. Geninasca; English translation by Gary Phillips to be published by Pickwick Press.

32. Cf. the journal *Sémiotique et Bible,* published by the Centre pour

l'Analyse du Discours Religieux (CADIR, 25 rue du Plat, Lyon), ed. J. Delorme.

CHAPTER 2

1. See esp. A. J. Greimas, "Elements of a Narrative Grammar," *Diacritics,* March 1977, pp. 23–40; and F. Nef, ed., *La Structure Elémentaire de la Signification* (Brussels: Complex, 1976).

2. A. J. Greimas, *Maupassant: La Sémiotique du Texte* (Paris: Seuil, 1976), p. 263.

3. Cf. D. Patte, *What Is Structural Exegesis?* (Philadelphia: Fortress Press, 1976), chap. 4.

4. Cf. L. Marin, *Sémiotique de la Passion* (Paris: BSR, 1971), chap. 1.

5. Greimas, "Elements of a Narrative Grammar," p. 29. The words within parentheses are ours.

6. What are called "idiolectal" and "sociolectal semantic universe," according to Greimas's terminology in *Maupassant* (see the several references provided in the index), correspond to what Greimas terms "ideology" and "axiology" in "Elements of a Narrative Grammar," p. 27. These two types of systems of values are represented in a static mode for the sake of analysis, yet they need to be conceived as dynamic. Through their dynamism they are capable of generating both non-narrative and narrative discursive forms.

7. As is the case with any new model it is subject to revision and refinement. But on the basis of our theoretical research and of the verification it has undergone we can affirm its operationality; the relations between discursive elements constituting this model are constants and can be identified in any narrative. It is, therefore, sufficiently established to be the basis upon which we can elaborate a method of analysis that will allow us to compare narratives in a systematic and rigorous manner in terms of a specific level of their meaning effects, the level of their presupposed semantic universe.

8. Let us note that the structure of the symbolic system will be fully determined only when we have considered in the second step of our theoretical discussion the relations that this system maintains with both the narrative system and the system of pertinent transformations.

9. This is in fact what we had unwillingly verified through our study of parables that led us to confuse mythical and symbolic systems.

10. In what is to follow, when we refer to the structure common to

both the mythical system and the symbolic system we shall write "(macro)-mytheme" in order to designate the oppositional terms.

11. For a more detailed explanation of this formula as we interpret it, see Patte, *What Is Structural Exegesis?* pp. 55–58, 61.

12. We shall see below how "state" and "function" may be defined in terms of the relations between symbolic system and narrative system.

13. Cf. A. J. Greimas and F. Rastier, "The Interactions of Semiotic Constraints," *Yale French Studies* 41 (1968); and "Elements of a Narrative Grammar," p. 25.

14. Cf. Lévi-Strauss, *Structural Anthropology* (Garden City, N.Y.: Basic Books, 1963), pp. 222–25. In the Zuni myth the deixis "death-war" is in fact positive. We represented it as we did so as to be consistent with our preceding theoretical example, which corresponds to the contemporary Western systems of values.

15. Several examples of this use of the semiotic square that elucidate the pertinent semantic features which form the value symbolized by (macro)-mythemes are provided in the structural exegesis of Mark 15 and 16, pages 62 and following. The readers should not hesitate to interrupt their reading of the present chapter to study a few of these concrete examples.

16. In a semiotic square we could say that this mediating term is the "complex" term which combines the contraries. Yet let us say once again that the mythical system can*not* be represented as such by semiotic squares.

17. The other subcontrary is the potential mediating term of an inverted semantic universe.

18. Other formulations of the existential opposition are possible, such as God vs. man.

19. Here, as throughout this work, the term "value" must be understood in the technical sense that F. de Saussure gave to it: it is the semantic dimension that a sign receives from its paradigmatic relations to the other signs in a given system. Similarly, the term "value" designates here the semantic dimension that a given element of the narrative system receives from its paradigmatic relations to other narrative elements.

20. Several examples of symbolic systems can be found below (pp. 62–84). The reader should consult these concrete illustrations before going further. We shall explain below why in a complex narrative we found several interrelated symbolic systems.

21. Cf. A. J. Greimas, *Sémantique Structurale* (Paris: Larousse, 1966), pp. 69ff.

22. In so doing we will move to a higher level of abstractions as compared with the presentation of the narrative structure in Chapter 3 of *What Is Structural Exegesis?* As a result, this new model can also be used with "logical" texts. Yet as a whole the former model remains valid.

23. We shall use the phrase "narrative program" instead of "narrative sequence" so as to conform our terminology with that of recent publications. In ibid., p. 37, we had already pointed out that these two phrases are interchangeable.

24. Cf. Greimas, "Elements of a Narrative Grammar," pp. 29–32. Greimas uses the formula ET $=$ F: transfer ($D^1 \rightarrow O^1 \rightarrow D^2$). We modify this formula (canonical form of the schema of communication) in order to make clear the link between this model and Greimas's actantial model. Let us emphasize that this model represents primarily a performance, i.e., a process (the transmission of an OBJECT) and not its result. It remains that the various actantial positions are semantically invested and thus represent specific states.

25. Our definition of a narrative program as *transformation* of the state of the RECEIVER implies that the OBJECT be conceived in a broad sense. An OBJECT is *anything* that transforms the state of the RECEIVER when it is attributed to him. Thus the qualifications, the locations, the temporal sequences, etc., will have to be viewed as investments of the actantial position of OBJECT when they are attributed to the RECEIVER even though they are not "concrete things" that can be passed from one personage to another.

26. In the representation of a transformation ($O \rightarrow R$), the arrow means "the performance has taken place." The symbol "$\nrightarrow$" indicates that the performance has not taken place and, therefore, that the transformation did not take place.

27. Examples of this minimal representation of narrative programs can be found on pp. 48ff.

28. The investment of the actantial position of OPPONENT also defines the state of the SUBJECT, as will be discussed below.

29. The end result of a narrative program is the transformation of the state of the RECEIVER. Ultimately it may in turn become the SUBJECT of a narrative program. Only when we consider this new program will we account for the result of a narrative program. The state of this new SUBJECT will include its qualifications as "having received the OBJECT" transferred through the preceding program.

30. Let us emphasize that we are speaking of *correspondence*. We do

not claim that the oppositions of the programs manifested by the narrativity must be assimilated to the oppositions of mythemes.

31. We use the expression "ultimate program" rather than "principal program" because it is not necessarily the one which is the most highly developed in the narrative manifestation. Let us underscore that the "ultimate program" is necessarily a completed program, i.e., a program which has been carried out successfully.

32. Let us underscore the fact that in all these remarks we shall refer to the actant and not to the characters of the narrative: the same character may invest different actantial positions in different programs.

33. The hierarchy of Mark 15:43–46 is provided as an appendix to Chapter 3, page 93. The symbols " + " and " − " designate the narrative programs that belong to the "principal" and "polemical" dimensions (or axes) of the hierarchy. Consult also the section dealing with "the identification of the narrative axes" of Mark 15 and 16, pages 45–48.

34. The "line" above a symbol (or a word) expresses that this symbol (or word) has a value contradictory to that of this symbol (or word) without the line above it. Thus "life vs. non-life" can be written "life vs. $\overline{\text{life}}$." Therefore $\overline{R}$ should be read: RECEIVER with a value that is contradictory with the value of another RECEIVER.

35. Greimas has proposed to represent each opposition of pertinent transformations in the form of a "square of transfers" (not to be confused with a semiotic square) in *Du Sens* (Paris: Seuil, 1970), pp. 176ff. We have not adopted this representation because it can account for only one type of opposition: $(O \rightarrow R)$ versus $(O \rightarrow \overline{R})$.

36. Let us underscore the fact that a pertinent transformation may be realized (attribution) or non-realized (non-attribution).

37. An example of a system of pertinent transformations can be found on pp. 52ff.

38. We must be careful here not to confuse the referential-denotative meaning of the processes with the symbolic values that, as we shall see, are manifested by the qualifications of the SUBJECTS.

39. As such the pertinent polemical programs constitute on their axis what could eventually be the simplified principal hierarchy of a polemical narrative. If this virtual polemical narrative were manifested it would include within its principal hierarchy the elements of the actual principal hierarchy of the existing narrative in the form of polemical fragments. In other words, the axes of the system of transformations are symmetrical. However, we must note that the formulation of the polemical programs is

subordinated in the narrative manifestation to that of the principal programs. Consequently, the narrative link among the polemical programs
is blurred.

40. We have arbitrarily employed the three possible manifestations of
the polemical transformations to make it clear that their formulation is
subordinated to that of the principal programs. We did not represent the
SUBJECTS so as not to anticipate the following comments. Let us note
that it is possible to study in a more precise way the relations between the
transformations as Greimas and his disciples have done in their research
on the modalities. The oppositions that we would consider in such a case
would be the oppositions of complex terms that we should break down by
isolating their elements. We do not do this here in order to avoid over-
burdening a model that is already complex. Also, it would not contribute
a single criterion for the method below. See Greimas, "Pour une théorie
des modalités," *Langages* 43 (September 1976): 90–107.

41. We must note, however, that the principal axis may correspond
equally well to either the negative or the positive axis, and the polemical
axis equally well to either the positive or negative axis. The positive or
negative value of an axis is not determined narratively but semantically.

42. This logic of the narrative development is *manifested* on the axis
of the principal programs but remains only *virtual* on the axis of the
polemical programs.

43. Greimas, "Elements of a Narrative Grammar," pp. 23ff.

44. In this theoretical example we presuppose that the principal axis
corresponds to the positive axis. In this instance the order of the positive
programs, since it represents the principal hierarchy in a simplified way,
determines the order of the negative programs. If, on the other hand, the
principal axis were designated by semantic indices as being the negative
axis, the order of the negative programs would determine the order of the
positive programs along their own axis. Since by convention we always
represent the positive axis of the symbolic system on the left, it would be
necessary in this second case to invert the order of the axes so as to pass
from the system of transformations to the symbolic system. Figure 8 and
its discussion are applicable *mutatis mutandis* to both cases.

45. A third graphic possibility would be to reverse the pairs of terms
along the negative axis. In this case we would no longer be able to understand the relations between the squares because those relations between
the terms of the negative axis would no longer be in a relation of ‘mplica-
tion. We shall see below the importance of this relation.

46. When the validity of all the other relations of the square will have been demonstrated, the other contradictory relations will themselves be established.

47. We shall presuppose all the while an example in which the principal axis of the system of transformations corresponds to the positive axis of the symbolic system.

48. Greimas, *Maupassant,* pp. 43–45, and *Sémiotique et sciences sociales* (Paris: Seuil, 1976), pp. 22ff. Whereas the relations of the narrative logic belong to the metonymic process that modifies the referential relation, the anaphoric process is concerned with the semic organization. For more on this distinction between metaphoric and metonymic processes see Michel Le Guern, *Sémantique de la métaphore et de la métonymie* (Paris: Larousse, 1973).

49. This does not mean that the SUBJECTS of the narrative programs that are found at the end of a complex narrative automatically manifest the most fundamental values. The interruptions of the narrative hierarchical pattern and of the logic of the narrative development (which will allow us to identify the subnarratives) break the semantic order. Let us emphasize once more that the model under discussion is only valid for an *elementary* narrative—a narrative with a single narrative level—i.e., in most cases for a subnarrative of a more complex text. We shall see below how to deal with the relation of the various semantic universes of the subnarratives.

50. As we have already said, these transformations do not necessarily manifest an explicit narrative hierarchy due to the fact that the opposed programs may take three different forms. Nonetheless, it is clear that these programs presuppose a negative hierarchy that we could bring into view by having the polemical transformations take the form of an antinarrative. That would require a reformulation of the transformations, but the SUBJECTS would remain the same and the relations between them would remain stable. Thus, in the parable of the Good Samaritan the performance of the robbers, which is expressed in terms of the man's story, could be expressed in terms of the robbers' story. Thus all that we have said concerning the positive SUBJECTS and the relations of implication between the states that they manifest is applicable to the SUBJECTS of the polemical axis.

51. We could also list here the case of the flashbacks that interrupt the flow of the story. Yet, they often contribute to the narrative development at an interpretative level and therefore may be either converging narratives or diverging narratives.

52. In such a case the further narrative development can be viewed as the narrative prolongation of both the original narrative (in our example, the Pilate-Jesus story) and of the intersecting narrative (the Pilate-crowd story).

53. What Propp called the glorifying test is in most instances a diverging narrative based upon an interpretation of the value of the hero's story.

54. These interpretative appropriations are often manifested by verbs of perception (e.g., seeing, hearing) or by verbs of cognitive appropriation (e.g., understanding, thinking).

55. Of course, in a very complex narrative we may find more than two narrative levels. The interpretative level may be the basis upon which a diverging narrative which belongs to a secondary interpretative level is developed, etc.

56. If several interpretative narratives are based upon interpretations of the same elements of the primary level narrative, they must be analyzed together; they belong to the same semantic domain (the same isotopy).

57. Let us emphasize that the ultimate program of an elementary narrative is the last *fulfilled* program of the narrative development. An unfulfilled program at the end of an elementary narrative belongs to the polemical axis.

58. A different OBJECT attributed to the same RECEIVER ($\overline{O} \rightarrow R$), the same OBJECT attributed to a different RECEIVER ($O \rightarrow \overline{R}$), or the same function interrupted ($O \nrightarrow R$).

59. In a long elementary narrative the narrative development may be alternately "commanded" by the principal axis (at the end of the elementary narrative) and by the polemical axis. In such a case the order of the narrative development is respected alternately on the principal axis and on the polemical axis. The organization of the diagram from the bottom toward the top is an arbitrary convention that will be presupposed in the rest of the graphic representations of the analysis.

60. Two branches can be attached to the same pair of programs of the primary level when one involves the interpretation of the principal program and the other that of the polemical program.

CHAPTER 3

1. It would be interesting to compare the structural exegesis of this text with those of the texts formed with the longer endings. We could then show the changes brought to the system of values presupposed by the "short text" by the addition of one or the other longer ending. This

study can not be presented within the limits of this methodological book.

2. The analysis of the rest of the Gospel would allow us to *refine* the analysis of our text because of its paradigmatic relations with other parts of the Gospel. But there is no reason to believe that such a study would contradict the results of our exegesis.

3. Verse 15 implies that Pilate has attributed (released to them) the OBJECT Jesus to the soldiers (collective SUBJECT of the program of crucifixion and SUBJECT of the program manifested in verse 16).

4. Following the results of traditional exegesis, we do not take into account verse 28, which does not exist in important manuscripts.

5. The interpretative process is not always manifested. This is why we cannot use as a criterion for the identification of the diverging narratives the presence of phrases (or words) expressing the interpretative process. Yet the presence of such phrases confirms the validity of the conclusion reached on the basis of the break in the formal hierarchical pattern.

6. It involves a few polemical programs, among them the last one, NP 7b, 8b: women (message $\nrightarrow$ disciples). The notation NP 16:7b, 8b should be read: Narrative Program manifested in verses 7b and 8b of chapter 16.

7. Despite the fact that there are two narrative levels involved, they can be viewed as forming a single interpretative level because the secondary diverging narratives prolong directly the end of the preceding diverging narratives.

8. At this point in the analysis the observation that one axis is more manifest than the other is necessarily tentative. It is simply a first approximation that attempts to determine which axis is the "shorter" of the two. An error in judgment at this point would not change the results of the exegesis (which would simply be longer to perform).

9. At this stage of the analysis, we need to keep in mind the "grid" representing a narrative program (cf. D. Patte, *What Is Structural Exegesis?* [Philadelphia: Fortress Press, 1976), pp. 43–49] even though we shall use a shorthand notation. While we do not take into account the qualifications (i.e., the investments of the actantial positions of HELPER, SENDER, and OPPONENT), we must take note of the narrative statements (CS 1, CS 2, DS, PS 1, PS 2, PS 3) manifested in the text for each program, and especially whether a program has been completed (i.e., if a PS 3 is manifested) or not. Indeed, any program (even an interrupted program) may be pertinent. Yet there is an opposition of pertinent transformations only in the case when one of the two programs has reached

completion (this completion may be expressed either directly or indirectly). Furthermore, the complete manifestation of CS 1 presupposes
that the SUBJECT is qualified with the will to perform the program; that
of CS 2 presupposes that he/she/it is qualified with specific HELPERS;
that of DS presupposes that he/she/it is qualified by his/her/its spatial
conjunction with a person, a location or a thing; that of PS 1 and PS 2
that he/she/it is qualified by his/her/its relation with one or several
OPPONENTS. These qualifications will be considered in the study of
the squares.

10. It is not necessary to present in detail how this reading of the text
is performed. It is necessary that the exegete identify the OBJECT attributed (or not) to the RECEIVER of each polemical action, so that
this transformation might be compared with the transformations of the
other axis. With some practice, this stage of the analysis can be performed relatively quickly without losing its rigor.

11. The asterisks designate the programs that "command" the narrative
development.

12. The personal pronoun that designates "the one who is wrapped in
the linen shroud" (v. 46) has a masculine form and not a neuter form
(as it would be if it designated the "body of Jesus," as is the case in v. 45).
In this way the text underscores the pertinence of this narrative opposition.

13. Let us note that the text does not manifest any opposition between
the centurion's attitude and the women's. The δὲ καὶ ("and also") cannot
be considered adversative.

14. Let us emphasize here that we should take into account only those
qualifications of the SUBJECT which have been manifested in the narrative development up to the point where the pertinent program is found.
The qualifications manifested further on in the narrative development are
not pertinent. Because of the progressive semantic investment of the personages, certain qualifications can be common to several programs. The
same personage can indeed be the SUBJECT of several pertinent programs. Yet in each program the personage is a specific symbolic expression which is manifested by a specific set of qualifications. Let us also
keep in mind that in many cases the SUBJECT needs to be in possession
of the OBJECT (which is therefore its HELPER) in order to transmit it
to the RECEIVER. This is especially true in the case of the cognitive
programs (such as the communication of a message); the SUBJECT has
as HELPER a knowledge about what he/she says. The location where
the action takes place and the time of the performance (if they are men-
tioned by the text) also qualify the SUBJECT. We shall record them

together with the other HELPERS. This is to say that we define the actantial position of HELPER as including everything needed for a successful performance. The identification of these actants is described in detail in D. Patte, "Structural Analysis of the Parable of the Prodigal Son," in *Semiology and Parables* (Pittsburgh: Pickwick Press, 1976).

15. We have given each narrative program the number of the verse to which it corresponds in the text so that the readers might easily consult the appropriate passage in Mark 15 and 16.

16. We do not say that the believer should attempt to incarnate these positive values. This type of hermeneutic, which is legitimate in the case of other texts, is not legitimate here, as will be explained in the following chapter.

17. The question of the manipulation of other people's beliefs (or better, convictions) remains open.

18. Let us note that the micro-system of values manifested by this semiotic square is not logical. We have indeed all the necessary elements of a "logical" square, but one of the contradictory axes (one "schema") is inverted. This can easily be shown by comparing this square with the "logical" squares proposed by Greimas for the modalities, such as the square of "willing to do" (A. J. Greimas, "Pour une théorie des modalités," *Langages* 43 [1976]: 90–107) shown in Figure A.

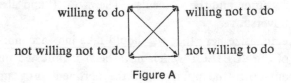

willing to do   willing not to do

not willing not to do   not willing to do

Figure A

Let us emphasize that the twofold negation is in the position of positive subcontrary. In order to show that in our square one of the schema is inverted, we shall represent the two semantic features of each term by arbitrary symbols so that the positive contrary term be represented by two positive symbols. The /imposition of one's will/, a type of will, shall be represented by "A"; the /submission to somebody's will/, a type of absence of will, by "A̅" (read: "non-A"); the /absence of power/ by "B"; and the /power/ by "B̅." With this symbolization, the third square can be represented as in Figure B.

The system of values presupposed by this part of the text is therefore paradoxical and illogical. But is this really surprising? We are dealing with the system of values that characterizes a faith, and not with a philosophical system! The manifestation of a paradoxical square does not contradict Greimas's theory.   On the contrary, the above analysis con-

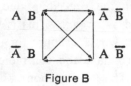

Figure B

firms what Greimas has often emphasized: the semiotic square should not be confused with the logical square.

19. This can easily be verified when /will/ is symbolized by "A"; /lack of will/ by "$\overline{\text{A}}$"; /power/ by /lack of power/ by "$\overline{\text{B}}$". The remarks of note 18 apply here also, *mutatis mutandis*.

20. F. de Closets, *La France et ses mensonges* (Paris: Denoel, 1977). See especially his chapter "Un silence de mort," about death as taboo.

21. This interpretation is confirmed by the study of the square which links the symbolic system of Interpretative Level II to that of the primary level. This square is identical with the seventh square of the primary level except for the fact that the term "Joseph" (NP 46c) is replaced by the term "Jesus" (NP 31b, NP 31c). Yet Jesus is qualified in these programs as "Christ, King of Israel," a personage in whom one must believe, i.e., toward whom one must have a religious attitude. Thus Jesus symbolizes a religious authority that must be respected. We shall not present a detailed study of this square (nor of the other squares linking the interpretative levels to the primary level); we would elucidate the same system of values as in the corresponding square of the primary level.

22. Cf. our remarks about the third, fourth, and sixth squares.

23. This conclusion is confirmed by the research of the "Groupe d'Entrevernes" (led by J. Delorme and J. Calloud). They note in the conclusion of their analysis of various passages of the Gospels: "The problems of competence and the manipulation of the modalities (will, power, knowledge) appear to be strangely emphasized" (Groupe d'Entrevernes, J. Geninasca, and A. J. Greimas, *Signes et Paraboles: Sémiotique et texte évangélique* [Paris: Seuil, 1977], p. 226. English translation by Gary Phillips forthcoming at Pickwick Press under the title *Signs and Parables: Semiotics and Gospel Text*). We can be more specific about Mark 15 and 16: the primary level of this narrative is a modal isotopy, i.e., an isotopy organized around the modalities.

24. We shall follow the order of the text for the study of the interpreta-

tive symbolic systems since, after all, the order chosen does not change the results of the exegesis.

25. We shall see below the difference between these two phrases.

26. In this square, as in the preceding one, the centurion and the soldiers could be designated as *pagan*. This is what traditional exegesis most often does. This term would account for the opposition Jewish vs. non-Jewish. We would then have the contradictory opposition /Jewish chief/ vs. /pagan chief/. This formulation, without being wrong in itself, does not show the pertinent semantic features that alone allow us to account for all the relations of the square. "Pagan" is a complex term that we had to break down into its two semantic features: /secular/ (non-religious) and /Roman/ (not a part of the Jewish society).

CHAPTER 4

1. Daniel Patte, *What Is Structural Exegesis?* (Philadelphia: Fortress Press, 1976), p. 6.

2. This new interpretative narrative level may be based either on the primary narrative level or on its interpretative level(s).

3. The above distinction between "sacred" and "profane" texts should not be confused with the distinction proposed by the proponents of the "history of religion" (also called "phenomenology of religion"). For such scholars (cf., for instance, M. Eliade, *The Sacred and the Profane: The Nature of Religion* [New York: Harper & Row, 1959]) the sacred and the profane are distinguished on the basis of functional categories. For them a text is sacred because of its religious functions, while another is profane because it does not have such functions. A text is termed sacred or profane on the basis of *extratextual* traits. By contrast we propose to distinguish these two types of text on the basis of *intratextual* traits, so much so that we can speak of the sacred or profane character (or even nature) of a text.

4. An "illegitimate" hermeneutic is far from being valueless. It is a creative use of the text similar to the poet's use of language. Because of its creative character an "illegitimate" hermeneutic may even be more interesting than a legitimate hermeneutic. Yet, it may also be the symptom of a conservatism that forces any discourse (and any text) into the stultifying mold of a narrow and static semantic universe. By contrast, a legitimate hermeneutic demands that the hermeneut accept the risk of perceiving the world and life in a new way—in the text's way.

5. We could say that an idea is transmitted metonymically, i.e.,

through the metonymic relations of the discourse (cf. O. Ducrot/T. Todorov, *Dictionnaire encyclopédique des sciences du langage* [Paris: Seuil, 1972], pp. 139–46). Let us also note that the realm of ideas includes what could be termed "moral values" insofar as they are accepted because their validity has been demonstrated logically (e.g., by a philosophical or theological argument). In order to avoid any confusion between "values-ideas" and values of a semantic universe, we term the latter "deep values."

6. Here we paraphrase Foucault (*The Birth of the Clinic: An Archaeology of Medical Perception,* trans. A. M. Sheridan Smith [New York: Vintage Books, 1975], pp. ix–xix) who has chosen as the object of his study "the conditions of possibility of the medical experience."

7. As with any other sign, the idea also has a value that escapes the control of the conscious thought process. In its relation with other signs, the idea is the symbolic manifestation of a value; it presupposes a value.

8. Cf. Paul Tillich, *Dynamics of Faith* (New York: Harper & Row, 1957), p. 12 and passim.

9. One too easily forgets this fact in our secularized culture. By over-explaining one transforms religious convictions into ideas and removes the power that they have as deep values, i.e., the character of signifying context in which lives and discourses can unfold meaningfully.

10. For more details about the Pharisaic hermeneutic see Daniel Patte, *Early Jewish Hermeneutic in Palestine* (Missoula: Scholars Press, 1975), pp. 11–127.

11. This is what Wink proposes to do by using the categories of Jungian psychology. Cf. W. Wink, *The Bible in Human Transformation* (Philadelphia: Fortress Press, 1975).

12. For more details about the Apocalyptic hermeneutic see Daniel Patte, *Early Jewish Hermeneutic in Palestine,* pp. 131–314.

13. A "type" can be defined as a biblical story (such as the stories of the Creation, the Flood, the Exodus, David) which is considered as the model and the promise of new acts of God in history.

14. Note that Jesus has certainly practiced this kind of hermeneutic. This would explain the freedom which Jesus had vis-à-vis the Mosaic law and the biblical ethical models.

15. "Gaze" (French, *regard*) is a technical term Foucault uses in *The Birth of the Clinic* to designate the way in which we perceive the world and human experience through a specific set of values.

16. As the authors of the *pesharim* of Qumran have done.

Glossary/Index

Brief definitions of technical terms are proposed here for the sole purpose of facilitating the reading of this book. Further explanations of these terms and concepts are to be found either in the main text (we simply refer to it by providing the page numbers of the passages where such explanations are located) or in D. Patte, *What Is Structural Exegesis?* (Philadelphia: Fortress Press, 1976), referred to as *What Is.* Cross references to other entries of the Glossary/Index are printed in italics.

ACTANT .... pp. 23–26
  Cf. *Actantial model. What Is*, pp. 40–43.

ACTANTIAL MODEL ..... pp. 23–26
  Component of the *narrative structure.* It represents the relations among six actantial roles or actants:

SENDER⟶OBJECT⟶RECEIVER

HELPER⟶SUBJECT◀OPPONENT
What Is, pp. 41–42.

ANAPHOR .... pp. 32, 120
  A specific type of *metaphoric* relation. Relation of partial semantic identity between two terms. One term (the anaphorizer) is condensed, expressing in a more direct and specific way the semantic feature(s) common to both terms. The other term (the anaphorized) is in a state of extension, expressing in a less specific and direct way the same semantic feature(s). The order of the two terms is arbitrary in the manifestation but ordered in the symbolic system.

AXIS (NARRATIVE) ...... pp. 26–29
  A *system of pertinent transformations* includes two narrative axes—a principal and a polemical axis—composed of principal and polemical *transformations*, respectively.

AXIS (SEMANTIC) ...... pp. 16–23
  An *isotopy* includes two semantic axes

—a positive and a negative axis—composed of positive and negative values, respectively. The *symbolic system*, as symbolic manifestation of one or several *isotopies*, also includes semantic axes. Each axis is comprised of the *deixes* of the *semiotic squares* making up either the isotopies or the symbolic system.

CANON .... pp. 100, 111–12
  Any *text* (be it *sacred* or *profane*) which is perceived as having an authority such that the hermeneut respects its semantic integrity even when this means that he or she must modify his or her own *semantic universe.*

CONNOTATION .... p. 3
  That part of the meaning (*value*) of a *sign* which has a "soft focus" and "blurred edges" but also the power to awaken the imagination because it manifests the symbolic dimension of meaning resulting from the interrelation of signs in a system that is reflected by paradigmatic (cf. *Paradigm*) or metaphoric organization of the content of a sign. [Vs. *Denotation.*]

CONTENT .... p. 7
  Cf. *Language. What Is*, pp. 28–29.

CONVICTION .... p. 6
  Self-evident truth (vs. *Idea*) that be-

129

longs to the plane of the *semantic universe* and is composed of a set of deep *values*. Because of its self-evidence, a conviction has the power to function as conditions of possibility of a discourse.

DEIXIS .... pp. 19, 32
Cf. *Semiotic square*.

DENOTATION
(or *referential* meaning) .... p. 3
That part of the meaning (*signified*) of a *sign* which is clear, precise, logical, and unambiguous because it refers to the informational content (information about concrete things, personages, events, and situations as well as about *ideas*). It is through their denotative dimension that signs are related syntagmatically (cf. *Syntagm*) and metonymically (cf. *Metonymic*). [Vs. *Connotation*.]

DIACHRONIC
A term used to qualify a methodological approach characterized by its treatment of a phenomenon in terms of temporal process. Should not be confused with "syntagmatic" (cf. *Syntagm*). [Vs. *Synchronic*.] *What Is*, pp. 13–14.

EXEGESIS .... p. 94
A type of interpretation aimed at describing and defining the discourse of the text, its nature, its semantic potentialities. [Vs. *Hermeneutic*.] *What Is*, p. 6.

EXPRESSION .... p. 7
Cf. *Language*. *What Is*, pp. 28–29.

FORM .... p. 7
The network of relations that organizes the substance of the content or of the expression (cf. *Language*) of a *sign* or of a *macro-sign* (according to L. Hjelmslev). This includes syntagmatic and paradigmatic relations (cf. *Syntagm* and *Paradigm*). In a narrative as macro-sign the so-called *narrative, semantic,* and *mythical structures* are components of the form of the content. *What Is*, pp. 29–30.

FUNCTION .... pp. 18, 23–24
Component of *mytheme* (or *macro-mytheme*). It belongs to the plane of the *symbolic system* (or of the *mythical system*) and corresponds to a *narrative transformation* on the plane of the narrative manifestation. *What Is*, pp. 76–77.

HERMENEUTIC .... pp. 94–112
A type of interpretation which involves the prolongation of the text's discourse into a new discourse (according to Ricoeur). The hermeneutic is legitimate when the *semantic universe* of the new discourse is compatible with the semantic universe of the text. [Vs. *Exegesis*.] *What Is*, pp. 3–6.

HIERARCHY
(NARRATIVE) .... pp. 23–26
In an *elementary narrative*, the series of *narrative programs* subordinated to each other by means of the logic of the narrative development and the formal relation, $S^1(O^1 \rightarrow S^2) \rightarrow S^2(O^2 \rightarrow S^3)$, so as to bring the elementary narrative to its conclusion (its ultimate program).

IDEA .... pp. 101–2
Truth established by means of a logical argument that provides a series of proofs. [Vs. *Conviction*.]

ISOMORPHIC .... p. 21
Isomorphic systems are systems having corresponding elements organized by the same *structure* and therefore identical in form. [Vs. *Isotopic*.]

ISOTOPIC .... p. 23
Isotopic systems are systems having corresponding elements organized by different *structures*. [Vs. *Isomorphic*.]

ISOTOPIC SPACE .... p. 30
The semantic feature(s) common to two contradictory terms of a *semiotic square* form(s) a semantic space to which both these terms belong. These features are qualified as *isotopic* because the terms to which they belong organize them in different ways, namely, by associating them with different sets of semantic elements.

ISOTOPY .... pp. 23, 116
The part of a *semantic universe* composed of an uninterrupted series of *semiotic squares* linked together because they manifest the same broad semantic category. A *symbolic system* can manifest several interrelated isotopies that are in *metaphoric* relation to one another.

LANGUAGE (French,
LANGAGE) .... p. 7
The universal phenomenon that characterizes the communication by means of a linguistic system of *signs* (French, *langue*). A sign is the relation between a *signifier* (*expression*) and a *signified* (*content*). Furthermore, a sign has a *value* determined by the relations of that sign with the other signs of the system and manifested by the *form* that organizes the substance of the content or of the expression of that sign. Cf. F. de Saussure and L. Hjelmslev. [Vs. *Speech*.] *What Is*, pp. 27–30.

LEVEL (NARRATIVE) .... pp. 33–36
Composed of *elementary narratives*. One needs to make a distinction between the primary narrative level and the interpretative narrative levels.

LEVEL (STRUCTURAL) ...... p. 15
In the structural network that characterizes a narrative, one needs to make a distinction among eight structural levels:

(1) The level of the *manifestation*
(2) The level upon which the *elementary narratives* and *narrative levels* are organized
(3) The level of the narrative system (hierarchy of narrative program on each narrative level)
(4) The level of the *system of pertinent transformations* (on each narrative level)
(5) The level of the *symbolic system* (manifested by a single complex narrative)
(6) The level of the *mythical system* (manifested by a society's set of narratives)
(7) The level of the idiolectal *semantic universe* (manifested by a given complex narrative)
(8) The level of the sociolectal semantic universe (manifested by a society's set of narratives)

MACRO-MYTHEME ...... pp. 16–18
Or "bundle of mythemes." It sums up the *mythemes* composing one of the *axes* of a *symbolic system*. Each of the poles of the oppositions of a *mythical system*. A complex unit made out of a *state* and of a *function* (cf. *Mytheme*). *What Is*, pp. 54–59.

MACRO-SIGN .... pp. 7, 9
Unit of the system of communication that is larger than a linguistic *sign*. Instead of belonging to the level of *language*, a macro-sign belongs to the level of *speech*. A narrative can be viewed as a macro-sign. *What Is*, p. 34.

MANIFESTATION .... p. 15
The text as perceived by the reader. The text as "meaning effect" "manifests" some of the potentialities of the *structures* and constraints to which it is submitted. *What Is*, p. 23.

METAPHORIC .... pp. 16–18
Two terms are in a metaphoric relation when they are interrelated paradigmatically (cf. *Paradigm*) through their *connotations*. We employ the term "metaphoric" to designate three types of relations: (a) The relationship among the terms that belong to the same *axis* of a *symbolic system*. They have in common certain semantic features (*values*) that characterize this axis. Such terms can therefore be substituted one for the other so as to emphasize the symbolic values manifested by a discourse (cf. *Anaphor*). (b) A similar metaphoric re-

lation can be found between a parallel narrative and another *elementary narrative* (the symbolic system of one is juxtaposed to that of the other). (c) Two *isotopies* interrelated so as to form a single *semantic universe* manifest another type of metaphoric relation. [Vs. *Metonymic*.]

METONYMIC .... p. 120
Two terms are in a metonymic relation when they are interrelated syntagmatically (cf. *Syntagm*), e.g., cause and effect, container and content belong to the same syntagmatic narrative developments. Such terms are interrelated through their *denotations* (or referential meaning) in a necessary relation, so much so that it is possible to designate the denotation of one of the terms by means of the other (metonymy as rhetoric figure) [Vs *Metaphoric*.]

MYTHEME .... pp. 16–18
Basic constitutive unit of the *mythical system* even though it is a complex unit made out of a *state* and out of a *function*. The *mythical structure* sets the mythemes in relation with each other so as to form *symbolic systems* and *macro-mythemes* (by contrast the macro-mythemes directly form the mythical system). *What Is*, p. 55.

NARRATIVE
(ELEMENTARY) ...... pp. 33–36
A complete narrative in its simplest form; it has a single *narrative level*; its *narrative hierarchy* is not interrupted. There are four types of elementary narratives: the primary narrative, the parallel narratives, the converging narratives, and the diverging narratives.

PARADIGM .... pp. 16–23
(a) Signifying unit characterized by a systemic organization of its elements. For instance, a system of *values* manifested by various textual elements interspersed throughout the whole textual development. A paradigmatic reading of a text is a "vertical" reading (and not "horizontal" as the syntagmatic reading is). The paradigmatic relations are of a *metaphoric* type.
(b) In a *sign* (or *macro-sign*) a series of elements of the substance of the *expression* or of the *content* organized by certain paradigmatic structures into a signifying system. The *form* of the expression and of the content manifests specific paradigmatic *structures* (the laws that govern the paradigmatic organization) as well as specific syntagmatic structures. [Vs. *Syntagm*.] *What Is*, pp. 25–26.

PROGRAM (NARRATIVE)
(or NP) .... pp. 23–24

Also termed "narrative sequence." A syntagmatic unit (cf. *Syntagm*) of the content of a narrative as *macro-sign*.

(a) An NP is made out of a succession of narrative statements constituting three *narrative syntagms* (the contract syntagm, the disjunction/conjunction syntagm, the performance syntagm) which result from the interaction of the *actants* in the framework of the *actantial model*. The contract syntagm establishes the relations among the SUBJECT, SENDER, and HELPER. The disjunction/conjunction syntagm establishes the relations among the SUBJECT, OPPONENT, and other HELPERS. The performance syntagm establishes the relations among the SUBJECT, OBJECT, and RECEIVER on the basis of the relations previously established. An NP can be represented by the grid proposed in *What Is*, p. 47.

(b) An NP can be represented minimally by the *narrative transformation* it brings about. When a SUBJECT attributes an OBJECT to a RECEIVER, the state of the RECEIVER is transformed: the RECEIVER is now qualified as in conjunction with the OBJECT. Thus an NP can be represented by the formula $S(O \rightarrow R)$. Cf. *Narrative structure.*

(c) An NP is termed "pertinent" when it involves a *pertinent transformation*. In such a case the qualifications of its SUBJECT (manifested by the investments of the actantial position HELPER, SENDER, and OPPONENT) correspond to a *state* (of the *symbolic system*). *What Is*, pp. 37–38.

REFERENTIAL .... p. 3
Cf. *Denotation.*

SEMIOTICS .... pp. 8–9
(a) The study of systems of signs. (b) The study of the phenomenon of communication in terms of a theory about the nature of signs. (c) The fundamental theoretical research upon which is based structuralism as applied semiotic research. (d) A given theory about the nature of signs. Any structuralist research presupposes an (implicit or explicit) semiotics. *What Is*, pp. 31–34.

SIGN .... pp. 3, 7–8
Cf. *Language. What Is*, pp. 28–29.

SIGNIFIED .... pp. 7, 101–2
Cf. *Language. What Is*, pp. 28–29.

SIGNIFIER .... pp. 101–2
Cf. *Language. What Is*, pp. 28–29.

SPEECH (French, *parole*)
Language as used by a person in order to communicate a message to somebody else (according to F. de Saussure). *What Is*, p. 27.

SQUARE (SEMIOTIC) .... pp. 18–19
A component of the *semantic structure*. Involves three types of relations: the relations of contrariety, of contradiction, and of implication. In Greimas's terminology the relations of implication are the *"deixes"* and the relations of contradictions, the "schemas."

STATE .... pp. 18–21, 24
Component of a *mytheme* (or *macro-mytheme*); symbolic manifestation of a deep *value* (or semantic value or again symbolic value) which together with other such values composes the *semantic universe* presupposed by a narrative (or by a series of narratives in the case of the state of a macro-mytheme); a state corresponds to the cluster of qualifications investing the SUBJECT of a pertinent *narrative program*. *What Is*, pp. 76–77.

STRUCTURE .... pp. 8–10
The structures studied in structuralist research (not to be confused with the "stylistic structures" of the *manifestation*) are constraints that offer their potentialities in quest of actualization to the author's creativity. There are three types of such structures:

(a) The "deep structures" (or *semiotic* structures), formal networks of relations which are universal in that they impose themselves upon any author and upon any speaker.

(b) The cultural structures or constraints (among which are the cultural codes). The sociolectal *semantic universe* is such a constraint.

(c) The enunciative structures or constraints, which are imposed by the circumstances of the enunciation. The idiolectal *semantic universe* is such a constraint. *What Is*, pp. 21–25.

STRUCTURE (MYTHICAL) pp. 16–18
A deep *structure*. The set of laws that (together with the *semantic structure*) governs the paradigmatic organization (cf. *Paradigm*) of the content of the narratives as *macro-signs*. It includes:

(a) The laws that govern the relations among a myth and its variants. Lévi-Strauss represents them by his formula:
$$F_x(a) : F_y(b) :: F_x(b) : F_{a-1}(y)$$

(b) The laws that govern the relations among the "bundles of mythemes" or *macro-mythemes* so as to form a *mythical system*.

(c) The laws that govern the relations among the *mythemes* so as to form a *symbolic system*.

At each of these levels the mythical structure (or symbolic logic) is the progressive mediation of a fundamental opposition by means of a series of secondary oppositions that admit a mediating term. The poles of these oppositions are complex terms, either *macro-mythemes* or *mythemes*. *What Is*, pp. 53–59.

STRUCTURE
(NARRATIVE) .... pp. 23–36
A deep *structure*. The set of laws that governs the syntagmatic organization (cf. *Syntagm*) of the content of narratives as *macro-signs*. They include:
(a) The laws governing the relations among *elementary narratives* in a complex narrative.
(b) The laws governing the relations among *narrative programs* so as to form a *narrative hierarchy* and a *system of pertinent transformations*.
(c) The laws governing the internal organization of each *narrative program* as signifying unit characterized by a succession of narrative syntagms and by the relations among *actants* according to the laws represented by the *actantial model*. *What Is*, pp. 35–52.

STRUCTURE (SEMANTIC) pp. 18–23
A deep *structure*. The set of laws governing the paradigmatic organization (cf. *Paradigm*) of the symbolic values (also termed semantic values or deep values) presupposed by a narrative or a system of narratives. It includes:
(a) The laws governing the relations among the four terms of a *semantic square*
(b) The laws governing the relations among semiotic squares so as to form an *isotopy*
(c) The laws governing the relations among isotopies so as to form a *semantic universe*

SYNCHRONIC
A term used to qualify a methodological approach characterized by its treatment of a phenomenon as constituting a system at a given time. Should not be confused with "paradigmatic" (cf. *Paradigm*). [Vs. *Diachronic*.] *What Is*, pp. 14–15.

SYNTAGM .... pp. 23–36
(a) Signifying unit characterized by the chainlike organization of its elements. For instance, a text viewed in terms of the logic of its narrative or discursive development (the textual elements form a logical chain). The syntagmatic relations are of a *metonymic* type.
(b) In a *sign* (or *macro-sign*), the series of elements of the substance either of the expression or of the content organized in a chainlike fashion. For instance, a narrative syntagm (cf. *Narrative program*). The *form* of the expression and of the content includes specific syntagmatic structures (the laws that govern the syntagmatic organization) as well as specific paradigmatic structures. [Vs. *Paradigm*.] *What Is*, pp. 25–26.

SYSTEM (MYTHICAL) ... pp. 16–23
The system of *macro-mythemes* organized by the *mythical structure* and manifested by a system of narratives as *macro-signs*. *What Is*, pp. 56–69, 61.

SYSTEM (SYMBOLIC) ... pp. 16–23
The system of *mythemes* organized by the *mythical structure* and manifested by a single narrative as *macro-sign*.

SYSTEM OF PERTINENT
TRANSFORMATIONS .. pp. 26–29
In a given *narrative level*, the system made up of the pair of opposed *narrative transformations* (each pair including a principal and a polemical narrative transformation) that are organized in the order of the narrative logic on the axis that governs the narrative development. (Cf. *Narrative axis*.)

TEXT (PROFANE) pp. 98–100, 105–12
A text whose interpretative *narrative levels* presuppose more fundamental semantic categories than those of the primary narrative level. It can be appropriated as *canon* as well as a *sacred text* can.

TEXT (SACRED) .. pp. 98–100, 103–5
A text whose primary *narrative* level presupposes more fundamental semantic categories than those of the interpretative narrative levels.

TRANSFORMATION
(NARRATIVE) .... pp. 23–24
Component of a *narrative program*. The attribution of an OBJECT to a RECEIVER represented by the formula $(O \rightarrow R)$. It corresponds to the *function* of a *mytheme* (or *macro-mytheme*).

UNIVERSE (SEMANTIC) .. pp. 18–23
The system of symbolic values organized by the *semantic structure*. In a given narrative the *symbolic system* manifests an "idiolectal" semantic universe. In a system of narratives the *mythical system* manifests a "sociolectal" semantic universe. A semantic universe is therefore

one of the enunciative or cultural constraints (or *structures*). It is the "conditions of possibility of a discourse" (cf. M. Foucault) or the set of *convictions* as self-evident truth presupposed by the text.

VALUE .... p. 3

(a) The dimension of meaning that a *sign* acquires through its relations with other signs in a given system of signs (cf. *Language*). Also termed *connotation*. It is manifested by the *form* of the content or of the expression of a sign. *What Is,* pp. 28–29.

(b) Basic component of a *semantic universe*. In such case it is termed "deep," "symbolic," or "semantic" value. It is symbolically manifested by the *state* of *mytheme* (or *macro-mytheme*). As a whole, the idiolectal semantic universe (composed of semantic values) is the value (cf. first definition) of a narrative as *macro-sign*.

VS.

Read "versus." Denotes the opposition between two terms (either an opposition of contradiction or of contrariety, according to the context).